Catechesis
for Infant Baptism

Ellen Marie Collins

Santa Clara University
Pastoral Ministries Program
Sheed & Ward
Kansas City

Sheed & Ward™ is a service of The National Catholic Reporter Publishing Company.

ISBN 1-55612-953-X

Published by: Sheed & Ward
                115 E. Armour Blvd.
                P.O. Box 419492
                Kansas City, MO 64141-6492

To order, call: (800) 333-7373

Contents

Acknowledgments

This book is dedicated to my family, Cherie, Julie, Tom, Joe, Tim and Katie for their love and support and especially to my husband Jim for his belief in me and for solving countless computer problems.

I am also most grateful for the help from the faculty in The Pastoral Ministries Graduate Program at Santa Clara University, especially to Sr. Anne Marie Mongoven, O.P. and Sr. Rita Claire Dorner, O.P. for their dedication, guidance and inspiration.

Introduction

The introduction to the *Rite of Baptism for Children* states that the "faith in which the children are baptized is not the private possession of the family, but is the common treasure of the whole church of Christ."[1] In baptism the whole Church is called to a deeper understanding of this common treasure – faith in Jesus Christ – and shares in the responsibility of passing on the faith to new members. In order to better come to know that this faith is a collective possession, baptismal preparation should be a communal experience. A baptismal ministry team is a vital link in that process.

This resource will help parishes design a catechetical process for the formation of an infant baptism ministry team that is inclusive and diverse. Parishes today often include members from many different cultures. The baptismal preparation team needs to recognize the rich cultural experiences within the faith community, and demonstrate great respect for the cultural heritage of those who come for baptism. And because many people feel isolated or unsure of their status within parish life, it is important for members of the faith community to reach out to them and make them feel welcome.

When families come for baptismal preparation, the baptismal team will provide a welcoming presence, a source of love and support for these Christian parents, and a challenging reminder of the responsibilities of profession of faith in Christ. The infant baptism ministry team will provide both a contact with the larger parish community for young families and a challenge to full, conscious, and active participation in the life of the faith community.

This program is designed to give parents an increased awareness of baptism as the sacrament of incorporation into the community of

---

1.   "The Rite of Baptism for Children," *The Rites of the Catholic Church*, (New York: Pueblo Publishing, 1983) art. 4. Hereafter referred to as RBC.

God's People, the Church. Through the activity of the baptismal team, parents will renew an appreciation for the role of baptism in their own faith journey, explore the symbols in the rite of baptism, and be encouraged in their role as the ones who will guide their children on their faith journeys. It is therefore vitally important that the baptismal team be knowledgeable about the Rite of Baptism for children, that they be aware of the paths of conversion they have followed in their own faith journeys, and that they have the skills necessary to effectively catechize these young families.

This book includes into three sections. The first section describes the process of catechesis with adults, with a particular examination of liturgical catechesis in sacramental preparation. This section examines the symbols of catechesis and the tasks of an integrated catechetical process. It also emphasizes the Rite of Christian Initiation of Adults (RCIA) as the model and norm for all liturgical catechesis.

The second section examines the Rite of Baptism for Children. This section provides an analysis of the Scriptural Lectionary for the Rite of Baptism for Children, the symbolic repertoire, and the prayer texts of the rite, including insights into the rite which are of particular importance in the preparation of the baptism ministry team.

The third section presents a process of catechesis designed to prepare people for infant baptismal catechesis ministry. The three sessions focus on the catechetical community as a community of believers, the symbols of baptism, the scriptural lections for the Rite of Baptism for Children, and the gifts of the catechist.

This work reflects the process of catechesis as taught in the Pastoral Ministry Program at Santa Clara University. The liturgical sections of the paper, especially the work on the RCIA and the analysis of the Rite of Baptism were inspired by Sr. Rita Claire Dorner, O.P. through her course in Liturgical Catechesis. The Catechetical sessions owe their inspiration to Sr. Anne Marie Mongoven, O.P. and the catechetical process she has designed. I gratefully acknowledge their guidance in writing this book.

The task of infant baptismal ministry is exciting and challenging. This ministry holds the promise of enriching parish life much as the RCIA has done. The challenge for the director of the program is to select members of the team with a variety of gifts, and to invite them to share these gifts and talents in shaping the baptismal catechesis. This resource focuses on the beginning stages of baptismal team ministry formation; however, baptismal team ministry is an ongoing process. May you make a good beginning!

ONE

Catechesis: A Lifelong Process

Sharing the Light of Faith recognizes infant baptism as a sacrament which involves the whole community:

> Preparation for the Baptism of infants is a "teachable" moment when the parish community can encourage parents to re-examine the meaning which faith has in their lives. In offering catechesis to parents and sponsors, the Church shows its love for and eagerness to support them as well as their children.[1]

Because baptism is a sacrament of the whole community, the entire community must be prepared to play a role. The catechetical process prepares people for the celebration of the sacrament and aids people in reflecting on the liturgical experience.

The baptismal ministry team represents the larger parish community by "encouraging parents to re-examine the meaning which faith has in their lives," as well as by offering love and support. Team members, who model by their lives the meaning of baptismal commitment, are a catalyst within the parish community. In order to best share faith and encourage ongoing conversion, it is essential that the baptismal team have a clear understanding of the nature of catechesis and a familiarity with catechetical process.

In this chapter, we will review the nature of and process of liturgical catechesis, using the RCIA as the model, especially as it applies to the Rite of Baptism for Children.

---

1. National Conference of Catholic Bishops, *Sharing the Light of Faith, National Catechetical Directory for Catholics of the United States,* (Washington D.C., USCC, Dept. of Education, 1979). Hereafter referred to as SLF.

The Nature of Catechesis

Catechesis is a lifelong intentional activity. Its goal is to dispose believers to risk continuing conversion to Christ so that faith might become living, conscious, and active. As described in the National Catechetical Directory, the goal of catechesis is to "foster mature faith" whereby people "constantly strive for conversion and renewal, and give diligent ear to what the Spirit says to the Church."[2] Through the direction of the Spirit, catechesis challenges people to renew their lives through ongoing conversion to Christ.

Conversion takes place in community; at the same time, members of the community is drawn into conversion through participation and reflection on the community's life and faith. The National Advisory Committee on Adult Religious Education (NACARE) names this process conversion *discipleship:*

> We can only be true learners, committed disciples of Jesus by allowing him to lead us to conversion. And, conversion is a lifelong process. Initial conversion gives way to communion, but communion, in turn, always entails successive conversions.[3]

This process of coming to conversion is ongoing and lifelong; thus catechesis must be ongoing and lifelong, always occurring in and through a community of believers.

Catechesis means "to echo or resound." Catechesis echoes the Word of God manifested in Jesus Christ. The preeminent source of all catechesis, therefore, is God's word fully revealed in Jesus Christ:

> Catechesis is trinitarian and christocentric in scope and spirit, consciously emphasizing the mystery of God and the plan of salvation, which leads to the Father, through the Son, in the Holy Spirit. Catechesis is centered in the mystery of Christ.[4]

God's presence is revealed in the lives of human beings through the power of the Holy Spirit in the person of Jesus. Jesus is the one "echoed" in the process of catechesis. All of creation and human experience in some way reveal God's presence in the world, and are appropriately a source of catechesis. Catechesis functions as a midwife, recognizing and interpreting God's revelation so that people might respond in faith.

---

2. SLF, art. 33.
3. National Advisory Committee on Adult Religious Education, *Serving Life and Faith: Adult Religious Education and the American Catholic Community,* (Washington D.C.: United States Catholic Conference, 1986) art. 49. Hereafter referred to as NACARE.
4. SLF, art. 47.

Catechesis begins with an examination of human experience, for catechesis is founded on the belief that God is present to us in our daily lives:

> Experiential learning . . . gives rise to concerns and questions, hopes and anxieties, reflections and judgments, which increase one's desire to penetrate more deeply into life's meaning. Experience can also increase the intelligibility of the Christian message, by providing illustrations and examples which shed light on the truths of revelation.[5]

Catechesis invites people to reflect on their human experiences and to interpret them in the light of the Christ experience. In *The Experience of God*, Dermot Lane suggests that:

> If we did not already know God implicitly in our experiences we could not even begin to raise the question of God. When we do find God explicitly in our experiences we are recognizing what was there all along.[6]

As a midwife, catechesis helps people look at the experiences of their lives in order to bring to birth the discovery of God's saving presence in every facet of life.

Maureen Gallagher suggests that the value of catechesis "is not to make the experience 'holy,' but to recognize the 'more' or the 'holiness' which is inherent in the experience."[7] Gallagher points out that the challenge for catechesis today is "to help people see that faith is an integrative part of life. It is the dimension of life which enables people to find meaning and purpose in everyday existence."[8]

The faith community provides the context for interpreting human experience. Through catechesis, the community begins to realize itself as a people, a people bound together in faith by our loving God. Through catechesis, the communal story of God's holy people – our Scripture and Tradition – is shared.

---

5. SLF, art. 176d.
6. Dermot Lane, *The Experience of God*, (New York, Paulist, 1981) 16.
7. Maureen Gallagher, "Forming Today's Disciples: Five Emerging Trends in Adult Catechesis," *New Catholic World* (Sept./Oct., 1987): 199.
8. Gallagher, 201.

The Tasks of Catechesis

The process of catechesis involves four essential tasks. *Building up the community* is the first task. Catechesis is always communal and has as one of its primary tasks the building of community, for it is in and through the community of faith that the meaning of human experience and faith are clarified. *The National Catechetical Directory* states that catechesis is situated "within the community of believers. The Church, the Body of Christ, is always the context for catechesis."[9] It is the community which catechizes. NACARE concurs in its report on adult religious education and the American Catholic community:

Learning in faith is not simply a matter between ourselves and God. As believers God comes to us in and through community. Our very approach to learning is influenced by the experiences we share with our local faith community and with the wider Christian community. We look to the faith stories of others both now and in the past, for insight into God's workings.[10]

Activities which serve to build up the community may take the form of welcoming activities, small group discussions, communal prayer experiences, and group projects on behalf of social justice. The catechist intentionally creates a process through which people come to different experiences of community.

Sharing the stories and beliefs of the faith community is the second task of catechesis. The faith story of the community, the Good News of Jesus Christ, is shared in dialogue with the human stories of the community. In baptismal catechesis, for example, the symbol of the water bath takes on new significance when experienced first in the context of human uses for water. The catechist uses the Scriptures for the baptismal liturgy as a source for discussion, reflection, and prayer, all with the goal of effecting a heightened awareness of what it means whenever this community gathers together to baptize in the name of the Creator, the Redeemer, and the Holy Spirit.

Praying together is the third task of catechesis. David Power says that "prayer is an essential part of the catechetical experience, since the whole point of catechesis is to foster a deeper participation in faith in an act of prayer."[11] All catechesis leads to worship; through the experience of communal ritual prayer people come to experience themselves

---

9. SLF, art. 60d.
10. NACARE, art. 62.
11. David Power, "The Mystery Which is Worship," Living Light, Vol. 16, #2, (Summer, 1979): 171.

as God's people, the Church, called to unity in love for one another. The catechetical process includes a variety of communal prayer experiences that incorporate song, movement, and gesture so that people are prepared to actively participate in the liturgy, and come to realize their important role in the liturgy.

Motivating action on behalf of justice is the final task of catechesis. In their 1971 document, *Justice in the World,* the Synod of Bishops affirmed:

> Action on behalf of justice and participation in the transformation of the world fully appears to us as a constitutive dimension of the preaching of the Gospel, or, in other words of the Church's mission for the redemption of the human race and its liberation from every oppressor.[12]

Catechesis is a ministry of the word in which Jesus Christ, the living word, is proclaimed and taught. It is centered on the person of Jesus Christ, who by his words and works – his life, death, and resurrection – affirmed the inherent dignity of all human life. Catechesis, then, finds its ultimate ground and source in the Paschal mystery.

Catechesis strives to continue the mission of Christ, a mission of love manifest in action for justice in the world. Such action must be given a central place in the catechetical process, which both motivates people to reflect on the need for social justice in the world and urges participation in activities which bring about that justice. It provides opportunities for people to become involved in justice activities and places before people the values of the Gospel, which both comfort and confront us.

The Forms of Catechesis

As stated in *Sharing the Light of Faith,* catechesis is "oriented in some way to the catechesis of adults, who are capable of a full response to God's word,"[13] and adapted to the faith life of individuals at every stage of development. In other words, catechesis is primarily aimed at adults, but it can and should be adapted for children and adolescents to meet their needs and their stages of growth and development.

A detailed descriptive profile of the parish group to be catechized is essential to the catechetical process. Such a profile enables the cate-

---

12. "Justice in the World," in *The Gospel of Justice and Peace: Catholic Social Teaching Since Pope John,* Joseph Gremillion, ed. (Maryknoll, N.Y., Orbis, 1976) art. 6.
13. SLF, art. 32.

chists to better meet the needs of the participants. A profile includes the age and ethnic background of the participants, as well as their family status, level of education, occupation, history of parish participation, and any special needs or concerns. The more information the catechists have about group members, the more readily they will be able to develop sessions tailored to their needs.

The Symbols of Catechesis

Catechesis interprets the symbols through which God reveals the Godhead to humankind. According to Karl Rahner, God's revelation is mediated through symbol: "All beings are by their nature symbolic, because they necessarily 'express' themselves in order to attain their own nature."[14]6 Symbols are communal bearers of meaning through which human beings make concrete the hidden aspects of their experience. Symbols are always open to interpretation, for they engage the imagination, disclose relationships, and evoke a response. Symbols transform our relationship with the world, with others, and with God by disclosing new ways of being and thinking in the world. God's revelation, mediated through symbol, manifests itself through the four signs of revelation: biblical, ecclesial, liturgical, and life signs.

Catechesis begins with an exploration of life signs or human experiences of the participants. The National Catechetical Directory suggests we begin by:

> examining at the most profound level the meaning and value of everything created, including the products of human effort, in order to show how all creation sheds light on the mystery of God's saving power and is in turn illuminated by it.[15]

Life signs include all the characteristics of the participants which are described in the profile, as well as all their lived experiences. These become the starting point for catechesis.

Life signs come into dialogue with biblical signs, one of God's other revelatory symbols, described in *Sharing the Light of Faith* as the "varied and wonderful ways recorded in Scripture in which God has revealed God's-self."[16] The catechetical process demonstrates how Scripture helps people interpret life experience. Scripture, then, interprets us, just as we interpret Scripture. It sometimes comforts, often challenges,

---

14. Karl Rahner, *A Rahner Reader*, Gerald McCool, ed., (N.Y.: Seabury Press, 1975) 121.
15. *SLF*, art. 46.
16. *SLF*, art. 43.

and always opens us to new ways of looking at our relationships with self, others, and God.

The ecclesial signs are said in *Sharing the Light of Faith* to be the "doctrinal or creedal formulations and the witness of Christian living."[17] By means of the witness of the Christian communities through the ages, the Creed, and the teachings of the Church – especially on issues of social justice – the Church helps people make their lifestyles more consistent with the life of Christ.

The liturgical signs include "liturgical celebrations and sacramental rites which mediate God's saving, loving power."[18] When the Church gathers to pray and sing together, to proclaim and listen to God's Word, to share bread and cup together, it is called to go forth and share Christ's love with others. In going forth, the Church becomes more truly itself. Through participation in the liturgical assembly, people are sent forth to bring Christ to others in their family, neighborhood, workplace, and larger community.

Liturgical Catechesis

Liturgical Catechesis prepares people to participate in the Paschal Mystery. It moves people to strengthen and deepen their faith by encouraging them to experience more fully the meaning of the liturgical symbols and rituals. Anne Marie Mongoven says that catechesis for liturgy is the ordinary pastoral activity in which believers reflect on liturgical celebrations, on symbols and symbolic action, on the nature of ritual. Thus it is in catechesis that the community prepares for liturgical experiences.[19]

The community prepares for liturgical celebrations by taking life experiences and setting them down next to worship experiences, in order to make clear the interconnectedness of liturgy and life and to better encourage participation in liturgy.

---

17. *SLF*, art. 45.
18. *SLF*, art. 44.
19. Anne Marie Mongoven, O.P., "Catechists and Liturgists: Can We Bring Them Together?" *PACE* 15, (1984-85).

The Rite of Christian Initiation of Adults

The Rite of Christian Initiation of Adults (RCIA) is considered the model for all liturgical catechesis.[20] *Sharing the Light of Faith* states that "full initiation into the Church occurs in stages. The Rite of Christian Initiation of Adults provides a norm for catechetical as well as liturgical practice in this regard."[21] The RCIA describes the underlying principles that should be included in any catechesis for a sacrament.

The RCIA demonstrates that conversion is a gradual process or journey that takes place within the community of the faithful in stages, marked by rites.[22] The process is gradual: It does not hurry the working of the Holy Spirit, but allow the Spirit to work through the medium of human time and experience. It occurs in stages, marked by rites. These stages resemble the stages of human growth and development, and the rites mark progress along the journey.

Catechesis for a sacrament such as infant baptism includes ritual prayer and reflection prior to the actual baptism, as well as opportunities for ongoing reflection that follow the liturgical celebration. Catechesis after baptism, like the *mystagogia* in the RCIA, provides families with the opportunity to celebrate and share their experiences of baptism. It allows people to discover together ways in which they might form their young children in the faith which they have professed.

The RCIA teaches that catechesis takes place in the community of the faithful. Article 9 states that "the initiation of adults is the responsibility of all the baptized." Thus, the entire community helps the catechumens and candidates through the entire period of initiation by their spirit of welcome and hospitality; by their full, conscious, and active participation in all liturgies for the catechumens; and by their own example of a spirit of reconciliation and love.[23]

The community is present in liturgical catechesis through many ministries. Those who participate in baptismal catechesis – including catechists, musicians, liturgists, and all who welcome and support the baptismal community – have a special role in guiding the parents by their example and support.

The RCIA demonstrates that the catechetical process is experiential and participative. Within the RCIA, catechumens share faith stories.

---

20. *The Rite of Christian Initiation of Adults* (Washington, D.C., United States Catholic Conference, 1988). Hereafter referred to as RCIA.
21. SLF, art. 115.
22. RCIA, art. 4.
23. RCIA, art. 9.

They listen to the Word of God proclaimed in their midst and break open that living word in the catechetical sessions. They experience anointing with the oil of catechumens, signing with the sign of the cross, scrutinies and exorcisms, and they participate in the public prayer of the faith community. Together with their sponsors, they participate in acts of service. Through the experience of participation in the RCIA, the catechumen prepares to publicly profess faith in Jesus Christ and to be baptized into the community of faith.

Catechesis for a sacrament such as infant baptism occurs through participating in building community; sharing stories, beliefs, and values; praying together; and taking action on behalf of justice. Through ongoing participation in these tasks of catechesis, the baptismal community is formed in the faith.

The RCIA teaches that liturgical catechesis is centered in the Gospel. The Word of God has profound implications for people's lives: It invites people to participate in the Christ event and to commit themselves to Jesus as a person. Participation in the RCIA provides a framework so that people might experience the Word of God proclaimed in the liturgical assembly. The RCIA is shaped by the liturgical year and by the person of Jesus Christ present in his word. In the initiation process, the catechumen begins to understand how the Church prays the Scriptures.

Liturgical catechesis, then, prepares believers to listen to the living Word of God proclaimed in the midst of the believing community. At the same time, it prepares people to participate in the symbolic gestures, actions, and words of the praying community. In the catechesis for a sacrament, a central place is given to the word of God. The scriptural lectionary for the sacrament is one of the primary sources for the catechetical sessions.

A further principle of the RCIA is that liturgical catechesis calls for a response in faith. Within the RCIA process of catechesis, witness, and participation in liturgy, the initiate makes a public statement of commitment to Jesus Christ. This public profession of faith is freely made, and is witnessed and supported by the faith community.

Liturgical catechesis for the *Rite of Baptism for Children* stresses the public commitment parents and community make in professing faith within the rite. This is a continuing and ever-deepening commitment that is a challenge to all the baptized.

Liturgical catechesis is centered on the Paschal Mystery. The RCIA specifies that the "whole initiation must bear a markedly Paschal character, since the initiation of Christians is the first sacramental sharing in Christ's dying and rising."[24] Through the RCIA, a gradual unfolding of the meaning of the Paschal Mystery is experienced in the lives of believers.

All liturgical catechesis bears this Paschal character, for as the liturgical year centers on the Paschal Mystery, liturgy celebrates the meaning of the Paschal Mystery. Liturgical catechesis prepares people to participate in the liturgy. It supports the conversion process by reflecting with people on the power of the Paschal Mystery of the Lord Jesus present in the liturgical assembly.

The Sources for Liturgical Catechesis

Liturgical catechesis uses rites – the public prayers of the whole Church – and their introductory notes as the basis for catechesis. The rites have a common ritual structure: assembling the community, proclaiming the living word, doing the liturgical action, and sending forth the community. Rita Claire Dorner points out that the primary sources for catechesis for a particular sacrament are the symbolic repertoire, the scriptural lectionary, and the prayer texts of the rites.[25]

In "The Mystery Which is Worship," David Power writes:

> Christians attribute all God's divinizing action to the Holy Spirit, God's power dwelling in creation. . . . It is on the basis of this principle that we can explain the use made in worship of material elements, such as bread and wine, water and oil, or of material actions such as the laying on of hands and other forms of touch and bodily communications.[26]

These concrete symbols of God's presence are available as a means of catechesis. Care must be taken so that the catechist does not attempt to explain the symbols, but instead includes an experiential dimension so that the effect of the symbol is experienced.

The ritual action of the sacraments is rooted in the scriptural lectionary for the rite. Analysis of the lectionary selections for each sacrament helps the catechist understand the theology of the sacrament. Scripture also leads participants to an increased awareness of the person of Jesus, whom one meets in every sacramental encounter.

The sacramental prayer texts are the public prayers of the People of God. A careful analysis of these texts illuminates for the catechist the meaning of both the action and the theology of the sacrament. The

---

24. RCIA, art. 8.
25. Rita Claire Dorner, "Liturgical Catechesis," Lecture, Santa Clara University, May 1988.
26. Power, 168-169.

sacramental texts are a rich source for prayer experiences within the catechetical process.

In sum, catechesis – a gradual lifelong process – leads people to experience the liturgy as a moment for celebrating faith and to encounter the risen Lord present in and to his people. Liturgical catechesis provides opportunities for people to make their faith living, conscious, and active.

An Analysis of the Rite of Baptism for Children

John Westerhoff wrote that "Ritual shapes our lives. To apprentice ourselves to the Church as the body of Christ is to participate in its liturgies, its symbolic actions. We humans make rites and our rites make us. No community exists without a shared story and shared repetitive symbolic actions."[1]

Catechesis in preparation for the celebration of baptism examines the ritual words, actions, and gestures, and reflects on their human meanings and their faith meaning. James Dunning writes that "catechesis is always about faith, conversion, transformation and never mere information."[2] The ritual words, actions, and gestures are not meant to be merely explained but also to be experienced in the catechetical process.

The catechist readies people to listen to the living Word proclaimed in the sacrament of baptism; prepares them to open themselves to the power of the symbolic gestures, actions, and words of the community gathered for baptism; and reflects with them on the power of the Paschal Mystery and its meaning for the community initiating new members. An analysis of the rite and its introductory notes *(praenotanda)* is essential for sound baptismal catechesis. In this chapter we will examine the introductory notes, the scriptural lectionary, the symbolic repertoire, and the prayer texts of the *Rite of Baptism for Children* in order to show how the rite shapes catechesis.[3]

---

1. John Westerhoff III, "The Formative Nature of Liturgy: Cultic Life and the Formation of Children," *Issues in the Christian Initiation of Children: Catechesis and Liturgy*, Kathy Brown and Frank Sokol, eds. (Chicago: Liturgy Training Publications, 1989) 154.
2. James Dunning, "Prebaptismal and Postbaptismal Catechesis for Adults," Before and After Baptism, James Wilde, ed. (Chicago: Liturgy Training Publications, 1988) 60.
3. Dorner, Rita Claire, "The Sources of Liturgical Catechesis," Lecture. May, 1988.

The Introduction to the Rite of Baptism for Children

The introductory notes to the *Rite of Baptism for Children* remind the catechist that baptism is a sacrament that calls people to faith:

> children should not be deprived of baptism, because they are baptized in the faith of the Church. This faith is proclaimed for them by their parents and godparents, who represent both the local Church and the whole society of saints and believers.[4]

The rite is revolutionary in that it emphasizes that the true meaning of the sacrament is fulfilled only later in life, as children are gradually formed "so that they might ultimately accept for themselves the faith in which they have been baptized."[5] The foundation for this faith is the sacrament itself. The baptismal ministry team clearly indicates to parents that formation in the faith is a serious parental duty; for the grace of the sacrament of baptism is stunted unless the child is allowed to be formed in the faith, surrounded by those who are models of faith.

The Introduction addresses this important role that parents play in the celebration of the rite: "It is very important that parents be present in the celebration in which their child is reborn of water and the Holy spirit."[6] The parents bring their child to a new relationship with God, as a child of God. This movement is marked by the public gestures and responses made by the parents. The catechetical process makes parents aware of the significance of their actions and responses during the baptism. The parents publicly request the sacrament for their child; they sign the child for Christ, renounce Satan and profess faith, and bring their child to the font for baptism. The Infant Baptismal Ministry Team needs to be prepared to help parents in this role.

Catechesis is always communal. The Introductory notes stress that the community must take charge of initiating its own members:

> the people of God, that is, the Church, made present in the local community, has an important role to play in the baptism of both children and adults. Before and after the celebration of the sacrament, the child has the right to the love and the help of the community. During the rite, in addition to the ways of congregational participation, . . . the community exercises its duty when it expresses its assent together with the celebrant after the profession of faith by the parents and godparents. In this way it is clear that the faith in which the children are baptized is not the

---

4.   RBC, art. 2.
5.   RBC, art. 3.
6.   RBC, art. 5.2.

private possession of the individual family, but the common treasure of the whole Church of Christ.[7]

For the catechists, bringing the community together presents a serious challenge. Catechesis for infant baptism needs to prepare the community to publicly assent to the profession of faith by calling the community into a deeper understanding of faith as the common treasure of the whole Church.

The child's right to the love and help of the community implies a serious responsibility on the part of the faith community toward young families. Catechesis should include the families, and might focus on the struggles and joys of responsible parenting as well as how we as a community pass on our identity, our values, and our faith as family and Church.

The Introduction emphasizes the need for sufficient time to prepare the parents and plan the celebration in order to bring out the "paschal character" of the baptism. We participate in the Paschal Mystery in a pre-eminent way through the sacraments. Through the sacrament of baptism, we are allowed to touch the Mystery so that saving grace becomes incarnated in us. We keep growing into the Paschal Mystery; we understand a piece at a time until all is revealed at the end of time. The symbolic repertoire, the scriptural lectionary, and the prayer texts of the rite bring out the Paschal character of baptism. The catechesis of the baptismal team, therefore, brings the community to a new awareness of the Paschal Mystery by providing opportunities to experience the primary symbols of baptism.

The Introduction to the rite is a treasure for the catechist who reads it critically. It is a vital aid for families preparing for the baptism of a child and for the formation of the baptismal team.

The Scriptural Lectionary

An invitation is issued to the catechumen in the RCIA: "You have followed God's light and the way of the Gospel lies open before you. Set your feet firmly on that path. . . ." Elsewhere the rite says, "You must strive to pattern your life on the teachings of the Gospel and so to love the Lord your God and your neighbor."[8] It is clear from the

---

7. RBC, art. 4.
8. RCIA, art. 52a, 52c.

RCIA that the way of the Christian is to be the way of the Gospel, and that all sacramental catechesis is to be rooted in the Gospel.

In the celebration of the sacraments, the word of God is centered in the assembly and shapes us as a people. As Catherine Dooley puts it:

> In the midst of this assembly, the proclamation of the word offers us a way of understanding our lives and our world from the perspective of our covenant relationship with God. . . . The readings call us to identify ourselves as the concrete sign of Christ in the world. In the assembly we are no longer simply a group of individuals but we are a people in whom Christ is present.[9]

Those who come for baptism gather as God's people to welcome new members into their midst. After the initial gathering, the People of God listen to the Word as the source of the sacramental action that will follow. As a baptismal team we must consider how to prepare people to listen to the readings. Active listening has to be a part of the catechesis for both the participants and the baptismal team.

Catechesis for the baptismal ministry team will include opportunities for the community to reflect on and discuss the scriptural selections from the Lectionary for the *Rite of Baptism for Children*. The team will consider the readings in relationship to their own life experiences, and will look at the Scriptures for particular implications for infant baptismal ministry.

The catechist for the baptismal ministry team must be well acquainted with the Scriptural Lectionary for baptism. These readings, critically examined, provide the foundation for preparing people for baptismal ministry. In order to analyze the readings from Scripture, the catechist begins by listing the passages from the Lectionary that are suggested for the rite. Then, the catechist critically reflects on the readings in order to identify the following: the literary form; the references to the symbolic actions of the rite; the images of God; the relationship of the images with the person/persons doing the rite; the theme of the reading; and other insights for baptism.[10] The baptismal ministry team will be guided through this process in a modified form here, but are

---

9. Catherine Dooley, OP. "The Lectionary as a Sourcebook of Catechesis in the Catechumenate," *Before and After Baptism,* James Wilde, ed. (Chicago: Liturgy Training Publications, 1988) 43.

10. Rita Claire Dorner, O.P., "Lectionary Study," Santa Clara University, Summer, 1989.

encouraged to continually reflect on the Scripture. Some of the insights from a critical reflection on the readings are presented here.

The Hebrew Scriptures

The readings from the Hebrew Scriptures (Ex.17:3-7, Ez. 36:24-36, 47:1-9, 12) describe how God's people were formed as God's own, and the relationship that exists between God and the people. The Lord God formed a people in the desert of the Sinai. God responded to the grumbling of the people by providing them with life-giving water. This water became not only relief for their thirst in the midst of drought, but the sign that God provides for them in all things. In baptism, we come to the Lord for life-giving water, which God alone can provide. This water is described in the Hebrew Scriptures as water for the people to drink, water that cleanses, water that touches and saves.

Through baptism we are forged into a people, who have been given a "new heart and a new spirit" (Ez. 36:24-28). In *The New Jerome Biblical Commentary* Lawrence Boadt says that this "new heart and new spirit" is:

> the seat of thinking and loving, so it will be a new way of looking
> at life from God's point of view. The new spirit is the power to
> live as an entire nation, not just as individuals.[11]

The Israelites were formed as one people, not simply a group of individuals banded together. They spoke and acted as one. In the life-giving waters of baptism, individuals are formed into God's people, the Church, and become one in Christ.

Ezekiel 36:24-28 concludes with the words, "You shall be my people and I will be your God." This is covenant language, the words God uses while saving the Israelites from the death and destruction of slavery in Egypt and forming them into God's own people. In baptism, all become God's own; rescued from the death and destruction of a world that does not know God, formed as sons and daughters of God.

Two themes emerge from a critical reflection on the Hebrew Scriptures used in baptism: the formation of the Israelites into God's people, and the importance of water in the life of God's people. Baptismal catechesis should include opportunities to reflect on the meanings of water for life, and the formation of the new people of God when they gather together at liturgy as the assembly of God's people.

---

11. Lawrence Boadt, C.S.P., "Ezekiel," *The New Jerome Biblical Commentary*, Raymond Brown, S.S., Joseph A. Fitzmyer, S.J., Roland E. Murphy, O. Carm., ed. (New Jersey: Prentice Hall, 1990) 325. Hereafter referred to as *JBC.*

The New Testament

Throughout the New Testament, the Scriptures speak to us of a new relationship to God through baptism, a relationship in which people are united by God into a community, a family in which all are brothers and sisters in Christ. The readings speak of sharing through baptism in the death and resurrection of Jesus (Rom. 6:3-5). In the *New Jerome Biblical Commentary* Joseph Fitzmyer says:

> The rite of Christian initiation introduces a human being into union with Christ suffering and dying. . . . The Christian is not merely identified with the "dying Christ" who has won victory over sin, but is introduced into the very act by which that victory has been won.[12]

The readings speak of being baptized in the Spirit to become one body in Christ (1 Cor. 12:12-13). Our diversity is rooted in unity, for we come to share in the "one Lord, one faith, one baptism, one God and Father of all, who is over all, and works through all and is in all" (Eph. 4:5-6). "Unity in faith may be regarded in this letter as unity of belief," says Paul Kobelski. "It denotes the teachings to which all members of the Church subscribe."[13] The baptismal catechesis provides opportunities to reflect on the one faith that we share, especially in preparing people to make a public profession of faith in the baptismal liturgy.

The readings describe the baptized as ones who have been clothed in Christ (Gal. 3:26-28), who are made more perfectly like God's own Son by the God who has called us, justified us, and glorified us (Rom. 8:28-32). The baptized are adopted sons and daughters of God who are "a chosen race, a royal priesthood" (1 Peter 2:4-5,9-10) who are anointed for service. A catechesis for baptism suggests service to others as the means by which one continues to grow to be more perfectly like God's own Son, and the sign of one who has, indeed, put on Christ.

The Gospels

The Gospel selections further emphasize the life of a Christian as one marked by service to others. The words of Jesus, "Live on in my love," (Jn. 15:9) sum up the themes of the Gospel. Three of the Gospel selections are centered on the greatest commandment, to love God and neighbor. Four of the passages offer examples of Jesus' compassion and love as exemplified in his meeting with the little children (Mk. 10:13-16), the

---

12. Joseph Fitzmyer, S.J., "The Letter to the Romans," *JBC*, 847.
13. Paul Kobelski, "The Letter to the Ephesians," *JBC*, 889.

Samaritan woman (Jn. 4:5-14), and the man born blind (Jn. 9:1-7), and most importantly by his crucifixion and death on the cross (Jn. 19:31-35). Baptism is rebirth into a new way of living, one that is marked by love.

The Gospels place great emphasis on the command to love God and neighbor; therefore, service to others should be an important part of baptismal catechesis. If love is the mark of the Christian, then any catechesis must include opportunities to consider the ways in which one can reach out to others in love.

The Gospel selections reflect an understanding of Jesus' life, death, and resurrection that his followers came to apprehend only after his resurrection, and celebrated as new members were baptized into their midst. References to water are found throughout the Gospel selections. Often water is connected with the Holy Spirit. In the baptism of Jesus in the Jordan (Mk. 1:9-11), the Spirit descends on Jesus like a dove immediately following his emergence from the water. Daniel Harrington comments:

> The opening of the heavens symbolizes the end of separation from God, and the beginning of communication between heaven and earth. . . . The Spirit comes with a dovelike descent, possibly an illusion to its hovering over the waters at creation. . . . All three motifs – the rending of the heavens, the Spirit's dovelike descent, and the voice from heaven - prepare for the identification of Jesus that follows, "You are my be loved son."[14]

In Jesus' discourse with Nicodemus he says that no one can enter God's kingdom without being begotten of water and the Spirit (Jn. 3:1-6). The water is living water which gives eternal life; it is drink for the thirsty, who will never have to drink again (Jn. 7:37-39); it is a bath that gives new sight and new life (Jn. 9:1-7).

This water is connected with belief in Jesus, who says, "Let him drink who believes in me" (Jn. 7:37) and, "Everyone who looks upon the Son and believes in him shall have eternal life" (Jn. 6:40). In the celebration of baptism, the ritual action of pouring water immediately follows the profession of faith. Catechesis for the sacrament should help people to see the connection between the public profession of faith which we make as the assembly of God's people and the ritual action of baptism.

Jesus is the predominant image of God throughout the Gospels. This Jesus is drink for the thirsty, light for the world, sight for the blind; the teacher who commissions his disciples to go out into the world to

---

14. Daniel Harrington, S.J., "The Gospel According to Mark," *JBC*, 599.

do as he does; and the one who lives on in his disciples. One reads of the works and words of Jesus which offer eternal life. The image of the Trinity is also frequently found in the Gospel selections, often connected with baptismal imagery. Catechesis for baptism should emphasize the Trinitarian aspect of baptism.

We are a Church of the baptized, a community of believers who remain connected to Christ and live on in his love by living his word. No differences remain among us: we are no longer woman or man, Samaritan or Jew, blind or sighted. All eyes are opened by unity in Christ. Belief in Jesus is key to baptism, but the relationship demands love of God and neighbor. Baptism in Christ is baptism into his death and resurrection. No one comes to Christ through one's own power, but only through the power of God. It is through God's gracious gift of love that we are formed into a people marked for love.

The Symbolic Repertoire

The ritual action of the sacrament flows out of the experience of the Word of God. Through an examination of the symbolic actions of the Christian community in *The Rite of Baptism for Children,* much can be discovered about how to catechize the baptismal ministry team. One begins by examining the human expression of the symbolic action. In catechesis, it is this human experience which gives the people a common basis of understanding. Everyone knows what it means to gather family and friends together to celebrate or commemorate meals, holidays, marriages, deaths, and other important moments of life. People know what it means to take marriage vows, to watch a public official take the oath of office, and to pledge allegiance to the flag, especially in the context of becoming a citizen. All people can relate to the rejuvenating effect water has on a person who is hot and tired, or the soothing and healing effect oil has on sunburned skin.

These human experiences begin to take on new meaning when examined in the context of the symbolic actions of the Christian community in their biblical and liturgical expressions. These expressions carry on a dialogue with the human experience, the one illuminating the other. Gathering, professing faith, and being bathed in water and anointed with oil come to be seen in a new way. One comes to a new understanding of the actions of the community in celebrating baptism.

This new understanding leads to a realization that one also has to live in a new way. Implicit in the gathering and the faith profession is a call to action. Implicit in the action of being plunged into water or anointed with oil is a transformation into a new people called to live in a new way.

The more fully people experience the human expression of the symbolic actions of baptism, the more fully will they experience the meaning of the biblical and liturgical expressions of the rite of baptism. The following section analyzes two of the primary symbols of baptism, the gathering of the people and the water bath. We will consider the context and the meaning of these actions in human life, in Scripture, and in Liturgy.

The Gathering of the People

To gather as a people is one of the fundamental expressions of human society. It bonds people together and frees them from the loneliness of isolation. People gather together in the presence of family and friends for many reasons: for celebrations of milestones such as birth, marriage, and graduation, and to support one another in times of suffering, when a member of the family is critically ill, or at the death of a friend or loved one. People gather for parties, picnics, and fun; to support teams or causes; to celebrate special meals together. While generally initiated by one person, gatherings signify the interdependence of all the people.

One finds many experiences of gathering in Scripture. In Exodus 19:1-8, Moses gathers the people together to prepare to receive God's covenant. The elders of the people speak for all, affirming the Israelite's desire to be God's own. The Sinai covenant is not an individual agreement between God and Moses. Rather, united as a people, Israel becomes God's chosen ones. God initiates the gathering and is present in the gathering with the people.

Mark's Gospel contains the story of the feeding of the four thousand (Mk. 8:1-10). The crowd assembles, Jesus blesses the loaves and fish, and the disciples distribute the food so that all may eat. Jesus initiates this gathering. He is present to the people first through his word. Then, through his compassion for their needs, he is present to them as they are to one another.

The Acts of the Apostles contains the story of the coming of the Holy Spirit upon the apostles (Acts 2:1-4). The followers of Jesus were gathered in one place. The Spirit filled them and they began to speak in foreign tongues and to make bold proclamations. The Spirit came upon them as a people, strengthened them, and opened their mouths so that they might fearlessly proclaim God's mighty deeds.

Liturgy gives us further insight into the meaning of *gathering*. The Church gathers as the People of God to pray and sing together, to proclaim and listen to God's word, and to share bread and cup together. The Church gathers to welcome catechumens and others about to be baptized, to celebrate marriages and funerals, to anoint its sick, and to help people be reconciled to God and one another.

The Church gathers to witness and affirm the sacred experiences of God's people. God initiates the gathering; we respond in faith. When the Church gathers together it becomes the People of God.

The Water Bath

Human beings use water in a variety of ways: for drinking, cooking, bathing, or to revive a wilting plant. Water is refreshing and lifegiving to body and spirit. Its cleansing power makes things new again. It is used to bring down a fever or, intravenously, to help sustain a life. The sound of a babbling brook or the sight of a waterfall refreshes the spirit.

Water can also be death-dealing. No one can live for long submerged in a pool of water. Massive amounts of water unleashed in floods can cause death and destruction. Yet water is so ordinary, so much a part of life, that we only notice when we have too little or too much of it.

Scripture contains many stories of water. God forms and orders the waters of the abyss so that they might bear life (Gen. 1:6-7,9-11,20). The waters of God's creation are to "teem with an abundance of living creatures" (Gen. 1:20).

By the power of God, the Israelites pass safely through the Red Sea, a wall of water to their right and left (Ex. 14:10-31). The crossing marks a passage from slavery to freedom, from death to new life. But Pharaoh's army is crushed by the waters of the same sea. The old way of living in bondage is destroyed.

Jesus is baptized by John, anointed by the Spirit, and acknowledged as God's beloved Son in the waters of the Jordan (Mk. 1:9-11). The baptism of Jesus marks a new way of living for Jesus – the beginning of his public ministry, distinguished by love and compassion for others and faithfulness to the Creator's will. Jesus is the new covenant.

When the soldiers came to Jesus at the crucifixion and saw that he was already dead, one of them "thrust a lance into his side, and immediately blood and water flowed out" (Jn. 19:34). Pheme Perkins comments:

> In the original story, these elements, flowing from the side of a
> victim, may have simply been the detail of a martyr story. . . .
> However, the Gospel has already interpreted "water" as the
> Spirit, which the glorified Jesus will bestow on his followers.[15]

Baptized into Jesus' death, we receive his Spirit and the promise of a
new life.

The stories of water in the life of God's people lead to the ritual
action of using water in the assembly of God's people. Water is used
liturgically at the beginning and end of people's lives. It is used in holy
water fonts and in sprinkling rites. It is used to bless people, homes,
cars, and wedding rings. Water is a symbol of new life, purification,
and our unity in the Lord.

The Prayer Texts

The prayer texts within the *Rite of Baptism for Children* are a valuable
source for liturgical catechesis. The ritual actions, gestures, and words
emerge from the roots of Scripture. The prayer texts speak powerfully
of the mystery of God's action in the sacrament of baptism. The baptismal
ministry team needs to take the opportunity to listen carefully to the
words of baptism, and to thoughtfully probe the meaning of those words.
The prayer texts may be examined by analyzing the "images of the
individual prayer texts in order that these images might serve as a basis
for sacramental catechesis."[16]

To Whom is the Prayer Addressed?

Most of the prayer texts are addressed to the community gathered for
the baptism: the children themselves and the parents, godparents, rela-
tives and friends. In the petitions of the community, Jesus is asked to
look lovingly on the people gathered and on all the baptized as they
pray. God is invoked during the actions of the rite: the blessing and
pouring of water, the exorcism from evil, and the anointing with chrism.
God's power frees the children from the power of evil as they are
baptized into new life.

---

15. Pheme Perkins, "The Gospel According to John," *JBC*, 982.
16. Rita Claire Dorner, "Analysis of Prayer Texts and Dialogical Exchanges As a Basis for
Catechesis," Class notes, Liturgical Catechesis, Summer, 1989.

How is God Named?

Throughout the prayer text, emphasis is placed on the creative power of God and the relationship a loving parent has with his or her children.

How is God Described?

The adjective *almighty* is often used to describe God, and there is great emphasis on the power of this almighty God to create and sustain all life, human and divine. God is also described as ever-living, the source of life and love, the giver of all life. God gives life and love to human beings and sustains a loving relationship of parent to the human race.

What Deeds of God Are Cited and Proclaimed as the Occasion for the Prayer of the Church?

In the sacrament of baptism, it is God who acts to bring the child into God's church. God uses the sacrament of water to give divine life, anoints with oil, frees from sin, and welcomes the child into God's holy people. God is actively involved in the sacrament. In the blessing of the baptismal water, the community is reminded that God has made water a rich symbol of grace. We are reminded that we are created in the image of God; of the deeds of God in the history of Israel; and of how God offered freedom from sin and death by sending Jesus into the world to give new life.

How Is Jesus Named?

Within the prayer text, Jesus is referred to as the Son of God and as Savior. Clearly, Jesus' mission is associated with the redemption of humanity.

How Is Jesus' Relationship to the Church Described?

The prayer texts constantly stress the redemptive activity of Christ, who cast out the power of Satan and rescued humanity from the power of darkness, the slavery of sin. Jesus himself accepted baptism and sent his disciples into the world to continue his salvific action: to teach and to baptize in his name. He has enlightened the Church and will bring all who are faithful to his word into the heavenly reign.

What Are the References to the Paschal Mystery?

The Paschal Mystery is referred to in the blessing of the baptismal waters, during which the prayer of the Church is that those who are buried with

Christ in the death of baptism may rise with him to newness of life. Elsewhere, in the prayer of exorcism and the prayer of the faithful, reference is made to the mystery of Christ's death and resurrection, and his victory over sin and death.

How Is the Spirit Named?

The Spirit is named as the Holy Spirit, your Spirit, and in almost every instance in connection with water. The Spirit breathed on the waters, at creation, making them the well-spring of all holiness. Water and the Holy Spirit are connected with newness of life, life in abundance that is given in baptism.

What Is the Work of the Spirit on Behalf of the Church?

The work of the Holy Spirit is to dwell within the hearts of the baptized, to anoint, strengthen, to bring about new life, to sanctify God's creation. As water is the source of human life, the Holy Spirit is the source of eternal life.

How Does the Church Name Itself?

Through baptism the church becomes God's holy people. We are brothers and sisters. Over and over again the Church is referred to as God's own children. We are the people who call God our Parent. We become God's children through God's action and our response in faith.

For What Blessings Does the Church Ask?

The prayers ask God to bless the new members of the community of faith with new life in abundance: to strengthen them, enlighten them, welcome them, keep them from sin and death, and watch over them at every step of their journey. It is as if all the energy of the Church is directed toward the children at this moment, as we cradle them in God's loving care. Parents, godparents, and the entire Church are to be models of faith and a source of strength for these children, and God is asked to bless the people in carrying out these roles.

How Is the Human Person Described?

The human person is described as God's new creation, God's own child. The community is described as brothers and sisters, the children as sons and daughters of God. Emphasis is also placed on living as faithful children of God, faithful followers and witnesses to the Gospel. As children resemble their parents, so these children – and all God's people – are images of Divine Being, temples of God's glory.

Insights From the Prayer Texts

Parents sometimes expect their children to receive baptism as if it were an object, a birthday present from God that one could neatly box up and place inside the soul of a person. Nowhere in the rite is there mention of indelible marks on the soul; instead, the ritual in every way indicates relationship. It is God who acts upon the human heart, who pours the water and anoints with chrism, in order to show that these children are God's own.

God is actively engaged in bringing us to new life. Therefore the catechesis for this sacrament must capture the spirit of the rite. The catechesis should involve participants in relationship with one another and with God. It should dispose them to risk conversion.

People must be actively involved in the catechesis. The catechesis should help people experience water, light, and oil not as objects but as symbols of the dynamic relationship, the love affair, that God has with humanity.

Because God is referred to as parent in the rite, catechesis should address the experience of being parent and enable mothers and fathers to find examples of God's love and parental care in their own experiences of parenting. People can then begin to realize that through baptism one becomes a member of a family, a brother or sister, a daughter or son of God. Baptism is not an individual action but a family affair.

The rite speaks powerfully of God's everlasting love and involvement with humanity in an abundance of symbolic action. Catechesis should dispose people to wholeheartedly experience this marvelous action of God. As catechists, we do well to give people eyes to see and ears to hear all the marvelous things God has done and continues to do.

THREE

The Catechetical Sessions

The infant baptismal ministry team is responsible for the catechesis of parents of infants to be baptized. In this model, two catechists will prepare the team for their role. During the first year that the team exists, members will develop a ministry of welcome to those wishing to have their children baptized, facilitate small group discussions during the catechetical sessions, and lead prayer during the sessions.

As they become more comfortable and knowledgeable in their roles, some team members may do more of the catechesis for the sacrament. Eventually team members will take an active role in the liturgical celebrations of baptism as greeters, lectors, and musicians, and perhaps will make follow-up visits to the parents of the newly baptized.

The baptismal team in this model is composed of six married couples and two catechists. For a parish averaging 200 or more infant baptisms a year, a larger team would be advisable.

The couples should represent the predominant ethnicities and income levels in the parish. At least some of the couples should also be parents, and a variety of occupational backgrounds will add diversity. Couples that are fairly active in parish life will make good team members, although newcomers can also make a great contribution.

Some team members may have previous catechetical background; most probably will not. But all should have some awareness of God's presence in their lives, even if it has been seldom articulated. It will be important for the catechists to enable these men and women to share their faith with others.

The process of baptismal ministry team formation can be accomplished through three catechetical sessions of approximately two hours each. The goal of the sessions is enablement. The catechists will help these men and women realize that through their baptism they have been given a great gift, a gift which can be shared with others.

The catechists will enable team members to recognize the events of their lives as the means through which God is present, and to realize that as believing people and (often) as parents they have much to share with those who are preparing for the baptism of their children.

The training sessions will focus on the following themes: The catechist as one who believes; the *Rite of Baptism for Children;* and how to share one's faith within the infant baptismal preparation program. During the sessions the participants will be exposed to most of the selections from the scriptural lectionary for the *Rite of Baptism for Children,* as well as to the primary symbols from the symbolic repertoire for baptism. Each team member will participate in leading the various prayer experiences during the sessions and will share responsibility for facilitating small group discussion.

Once the program is underway, periodic meetings of the entire baptismal ministry team will insure that the program is meeting the needs of the team and of the people who come to the parish for baptismal preparation. A copy of the profile of those who participate in the baptismal preparation program will be given to each member of the team so that they might better come to understand the special needs which this baptismal ministry team will have to address in the months ahead.

Session One:
The Catechist Is One Who Believes

Environment: The session may take place in any comfortable room used for parish meetings. You will need enough room for six movable tables which will be used during group discussions and activities. Arrange comfortable chairs around the six tables.

Place a round table covered with a white cloth in a prominent spot. Place a large white candle and a Bible on it. This table will be the focal point for all of the prayer experiences.

Objectives: The Catechetical Process:
Builds Community:

> Invites team members to become acquainted through a community building activity;

> Encourages people to share in small groups some of their life experiences;

Explores baptismal ministry as a communal process facilitated by the baptismal ministry team;

Shares Stories, Beliefs, and Values:

Encourages participants to reflect on the life experiences that have made them aware of the presence or absence of God in their lives;

Enables the team to recognize that they are believers; members of a believing community, the Church, who, through baptism, have been empowered by Christ;

Invites team members to reflect on and discuss the images of light and belief in the Gospel of John 9:1-41 – Jesus cures a blind man;

Prays Together:

Provides opportunities for the baptismal team to gather as a community of believers to pray and sing together;

Commissions the members of the baptismal ministry team through a service of light;

Invites different members of the baptismal ministry team to actively participate in the prayer experiences as readers;

Motivates to Service:

Identifies ways in which the baptismal team will help members of the parish community through the ministry of baptismal catechesis;

Suggests ways in which team members can encourage and support one another in baptismal ministry;

Experiences this ministry team as a community of believers empowered by Christ and commissioned to share faith with others.

Welcome: The two catechists welcome the Baptismal team members as they arrive. The catechists provide name tags for each of the participants and encourage them to partake of coffee and refreshments and to mingle as a group. When all have arrived, the facilitating catechist (one catechist may lead throughout, or the two may alternate leadership) invites everyone to introduce himself/herself. The catechist uses a community-building activity to help the group become better acquainted. The participants are given ten minutes to complete the activity.

Community Building Activity

Below is a list of ten questions. You have ten minutes to mingle among the baptismal team members to ask the questions. Write the name of each person interviewed next to the question he/she was asked and his/her response. Once you have written down a response for the person, you must move to another person. You may only ask one question per person. Since there are more members of the baptismal team than there are questions, you may have to work your way through the question list a couple of times. Your objective is to mingle with everyone and to learn something about each person that you did not know before.

1. What is the name of the last book you read?
   Would you recommend it?

   _____

   _____

2. What is the most interesting place you've visited?

   _____

   _____

3. Name something you did for which you are proud.

   _____

   _____

4. In what ways are you artistic, musical, or athletic?

   _____

   _____

5. Name your favorite food and restaurant.

   _____

   _____

6. What was the last movie that you saw. How would you rate it?

   _____

   _____

7. In your home, what room are you most attracted to, feel comfortable in?

   _____

   _____

8. What incident in your life had a great effect on you? Why?

_____

_____

9. What is your hobby; what do you do for leisure?

_____

_____

10. What attracted you to baptismal ministry?

_____

_____

Gathering Prayer: At the conclusion of the activity the catechist invites people to gather around the prayer table. The catechist moves to the prayer table, lights the candle, and leads with a gathering prayer.

Catechist 1: Creator God, You are ever loving and faithful, the source of all life.

Through Jesus Your Son, You have made the everlasting promise to share Your life forever.

Through the Spirit, the gift of Your Son, You impart new life on all who believe.

Through the Church, the people You call to faith, You embrace others with Your life.

Help us to reflect by our lives an awareness and appreciation of Your presence and promise.[1]

Grant us an increase of faith so that we might live out the promise of our baptism.

May our example lead others to You, and may we serve you, our living and true God, forever and ever.

All: Amen.

Catechist 2: A reading from the book of Ezekiel.

For I will take you away from among the nations, gather you from among all the foreign lands, and bring you back to your own land. I will sprinkle clean water upon you to cleanse you from all your impurities, and from all your idols I will cleanse you. I will give you a new heart and place a new spirit within you, taking from your

---

1.   Joan Brady, William Koplik, *We Celebrate Baptism: Program Director's Manual,* (Morristown, N.J.: Silver Burdett, 1983) 29.

bodies your stony hearts and giving you natural hearts. I will put my spirit within you and make you live by my statutes, careful to observe my decrees. You shall live in the land I gave your ancestors; you shall be my people, and I will be your God (Ez. 36:24-28).
This is the word of the Lord.

All: Thanks be to God.
A moment of silence follows.
The catechist invites the baptismal team to join in singing a gathering hymn.

When the singing is over people move to their places at tables.

Consideration of a Human Experience: (Lifeline Activity)[2]

Each person is given a sheet of paper on which a lifeline with numbers from 0 to 99 has been drawn. Participants are given the following instructions.

Draw a line that shows the major peaks and valleys (high and low points) in your life from birth to the present.

Describe with words or symbols the key experiences of these peaks and valleys.

The participants reflect individually on the key experiences of their life in relation to the following question.

How did these significant moments involve a change in your life? Growth? Reassessment? Re-evaluation? Clarification of values? Denial? After sufficient time to reflect on life experiences, the catechist invites team members to form two small discussion groups. Each person in the group is asked to share one of the key experiences of his or her life, and any insights he or she might have about its significance. If time permits, the group may share additional life experiences within the small group.

After sufficient time to reflect on life experiences, the catechist invites team members to form two small discussion groups. Each person in the group is asked to share one of the key experiences of his or her life, and any insights he or she might have about its significance. If time permits, the group may share additional life experiences within the small group.

---

2. Jeanne Tighe and Karen Szentkeresti, *Rethinking Adult Religious Education: A Practical Parish Guide,* (New Jersey: Paulist, 1986) 37.

Faith Reflection: The catechist directs the attention of the team members once more to the timeline. Each individual is asked to describe with words or symbols the times in life when she or he experienced a profound sense of the presence or absence of God. The participants then share one of these religious experiences with the rest of the small group. Participants are then invited to discuss what these experiences tell them about how people come to believe.

The catechist then says: "The Scripture offers many examples of people who have faith. The New Testament, especially, has stories of people who put their faith in Jesus. One such story is the story of the man born blind, found in the Gospel of John (John 9:1-41). This Gospel is a selection from the scriptural lectionary for *The Rite of Baptism for Children.*"

The catechist invites the baptismal community to watch and listen to a dramatic presentation of the Gospel. One person from the parish RCIA team has been invited to help the catechist with the presentation. The Gospel has been scripted for three voices; Jesus, the narrator, and the man born blind. At the beginning of the narration, six unlighted candles are placed behind the blind man, while six lighted candles are placed behind the narrator, representing the Pharisees – those who think they have the light. The Paschal candle stands behind Jesus, who is in the center.

Narr: A Reading from the Holy Gospel According to John. (Jn. 9:1-41)[3]

Narr: As Jesus passed by, he saw a man blind from his birth. His disciples asked him, "Rabbi, who sinned, this man or his parents, that he was born blind?"

Jesus: It was not that this man sinned, or his parents, but that the works of God might be made manifest in him. We must work the works of him who sent me, while it is day; night comes, when no one can work. As long as I am in the world, I am the light of the world.

---

3. A special thanks to Anne Marie Mongoven, O.P., for her help in scripting the dramatic presentation of the Gospel. This intepretation is based on Raymond Brown's *The Gospel According to John (i-xii)* (Garden City, NY: Doubleday, 1966.): 370-382.

Light Paschal Candle

Narr: As He said this, he spat on the ground and made clay of the spittle and anointed the man's eyes with the clay. . .

Jesus: Go wash in the pool of Siloam.

Narr: This name means "one who has been sent." So the man went off and washed, and came back able to see.

Person 1 lights one candle from the Paschal candle. Narrator pauses while candles are lighted or unlighted.

Person 1: Come to him and receive his light.

All: Receive his light.

Narr: The neighbors and those who had seen him before as a beggar, said: "Is not this the man who used to sit and beg?" Some people were claiming it was he; others maintained it was only someone who looked like him.

Man: I am the man.

Narr: How were your eyes opened?

Man: The man called Jesus made clay and anointed my eyes and said to me, "Go to Siloam and wash;" so I went and washed and received my sight.

Person 2 lights second candle from the Paschal candle, then says:

Person 2: Come to him and receive his light.

All: Receive his light.

Narr: Where is he?

Man: I have no idea.

Narr: Next they took the man who had been born blind to the Pharisees. Now it was the Sabbath when Jesus made the clay and opened his eyes. The Pharisees again asked him how he had received his sight.

Man: He put clay on my eyes, and I washed, and I see.

Person 3 lights third candle, then says:

Person 3: Come to him and receive his light.

All: Receive his light.

Narr: This prompted some of the Pharisees to assert, "This man is not from God, for he does not keep the Sabbath." Others objected: "If someone is a sinner, how can they perform signs like these?" They were sharply divided over him. Then they addressed the blind man again: "Since it was your eyes he opened, what do you have to say about him?"

Extinguish one candle from the Pharisee side.

Man: He is a prophet.

Person 4 lights fourth candle, then says:

Person 4: Come to him and receive his light.

All: Receive his light.

Narr: The Jews did not believe that he had been blind and that he had received his sight, until they called the parents of the man who had received his sight, and asked them,

Extinguish one candle from the Pharisee side.

Narr: "Is this your son, who you say was born blind? How then does he now see?" His parents answered, "We know that this is our son, and that he was born blind; but how he now sees we do not know, nor do we know who opened his eyes. Ask him; he is of age, he will speak for himself." His parents said this because they feared the Jews, for the Jews had already agreed that if anyone should confess him to be the Christ he was put out of the synagogue. Therefore his parents said, "He is of age, ask him." So for the second time they called for the man who had been blind, and said to him, "Give God the praise; we know that this man is a sinner."

Extinguish one candle from the Pharisee side.

Man: Whether he is a sinner, I do not know; one thing I know is that though I was blind, now I see.

Person 5 lights fifth candle, then says:

Person 5: Come to him and receive his light.

All: Receive his light.

Narr: What did he do to you? How did he open your eyes?

Man: I have told you already, and you would not listen. Why do you want to hear it again? Do you too want to become his disciples?

Narr: And they reviled him saying: "You are the one who is that man's disciple, but we are disciples of Moses. We know that God has spoken to Moses, but as for this man, we do not know where he comes from."

Extinguish one candle from the Pharisee side.

Man: Why this is a marvel! You do not know where he comes from, and yet he opened my eyes. We know that God does not listen to sinners, but if anyone is a worshiper of God and does his will, God listens to him. Never since the world began has it been heard that anyone opened the eyes of a man born blind. If this man were not from God, he could do nothing."

Narr: "What!" the Pharisees exclaimed, "You are steeped in sin from your birth, and you are lecturing us?" With that they threw him out bodily.

Extinguish one candle from the Pharisee side.

Jesus heard that they had cast him out, and having found him, he said,

Jesus: Do you believe in the Son of Man?

Man: And who is he, sir, that I may believe in him?

Jesus: You have seen him and it is he who speaks to you.

Man: Lord, I believe.

Narr: And he bowed down to worship him.

Person 6 lights the sixth candle, then says:

Person 6: Come to him and receive his light.

All: Receive his light.

Narr: Jesus then said:

Jesus: For judgment I came into this world, that those who do not see may see, and that those who see may become blind.

Narr: Some of the Pharisees near him heard this, and they said to him, "You are not calling us blind, are you?"

Extinguish one candle from the Pharisee side.

Jesus: If you were blind, there would be no sin in that. 'But we see,' you say and your sin remains.

Narr: This is the Gospel of the Lord.

All: Praise to you, Lord Jesus Christ.

At the conclusion of the Gospel, team members rejoin their small groups to discuss the following questions.

What does this Gospel story have to say about light and darkness?

What does it say about belief in Christ?

How does belief in Christ give light to our daily experiences?

How does belief in Christ help us to see?

In what ways am I like the man born blind? Like the Pharisees?

In what ways is a catechist like the man born blind?

The catechist brings the small groups together and ask for a summary of the group discussion. A short break follows.

At the end of the break, the catechist asks group members how they would describe a believer. When the discussion concludes, the catechist presents the group with the following list of characteristics of a believer. The participants are asked to compare this list with the characteristics they have noted. They are invited to add their own perspectives to this list.

A believer has a relationship with God.

A believer is searching to know God.

A believer is responding to God.

A believer is one who risks.

A believer lives out the gift of life God has given us

A believer says "Yes" to God's call.

A believer is trusting.

A believer lets go.

A believer is willing to ask questions.

A believer is willing not to have all the answers.

A believer looks past his or her own weaknesses.[4]

Action on Behalf of Justice: The catechist says, "A catechist is a believer; one who has been enlightened by Christ. Just as the man born blind was transformed by Christ, the catechist is one being transformed by belief in Christ. Just as the man born blind told everyone his good news of recovered sight, the catechist shares the good news of Christ's light with others. The infant baptismal ministry team of our parish is a community of believers. We have been given the gift of sight which is faith in Jesus Christ. The early Church called this gift *enlightenment.* We, as believers, are now commissioned to share Christ's light with others, and in a special way through baptismal catechesis."

The group then discusses the following questions:

As believers, how are you going to help others see?

Why have we come together? What is a baptismal ministry team? What is our ministry?

As a baptismal ministry team, how will we bring light to others?

As a community of faith, in what ways can we support one another in this ministry? How can each of us help to build up the ministry team?

Closing Prayer: The catechist invites the group to gather once more around the prayer table. Lighted candles for all the baptismal team members have been added around the large candle. Some members of the group have been designated to read.

Leader: We gather together O Lord, as your people who have been brought by the gift of faith out of darkness into your light. We believe in you, Lord Jesus Christ. Empowered by your light, may we go forth to bring your light to others.

Leader: As your name is called please come to the prayer table to receive a lighted candle. The response will be, "Receive the light of Christ."

Leader: *Name,* Come to Christ and receive his light!

All: Receive the light of Christ.

---

4. Brian Reynolds, *A Chance to Serve: Peer Ministers Handbook,* (Winona, Mn.: St. Mary's Press, 1984) 36.

Reader: As long as I am in the world, I am the light of the world.

Leader: *Name,* Come to Christ and receive his light.

All: Receive the light of Christ.

Reader: He spat on the ground, made clay of the spittle, and anointed the man's eyes with the clay. He said, "Go, wash in the pool of Siloam" So he went and washed and came back seeing.

Leader: *Name,* Come to Christ and receive his light.

All: Receive the light of Christ.

Reader: "He put clay on my eyes, and I washed, and I see."

Leader: Name, Come to Christ and receive his light.

All: Receive the light of Christ.

Reader: "Whether he is a sinner, I do not know; one thing I know, that though I was blind, now I see."

Leader: Name, Come to Christ and receive his light.

All: Receive the light of Christ.

Reader: "Never since the world began has it been heard that anyone opened the eyes of a man born blind. If this man were not from God, he could do nothing."

Leader: *Name,* Come to Christ and receive his light.

All: Receive the light of Christ.

Reader: "Do you believe in the Son of Man?
"And who is he, sir, that I may believe in him?"
"You have seen him, and it is he who speaks to you."
"Lord, I believe."

Leader: *Name,* Come to Christ and receive his light.

All: Receive the light of Christ.

Reader: "For judgment I came into this world, that those who do not see may see and that those who see may become blind." (Jn. 9:1-39)

Leader: *Name,* Come to Christ and receive his light.

All: Receive the light of Christ.

Reader: "You are like light for the whole world. No one lights a lamp and puts it under a bowl; instead, he or she puts it on the lampstand, where it gives light for everyone in the house" (Mt. 5:13,15).

Leader: *Name,* Come to Christ and receive his light.

All: Receive the light of Christ.

Leader: This light is entrusted to you to be kept burning brightly. You have been enlightened by Christ. Walk always as a child of the light and keep the flame of faith alive in your heart. When the Lord comes may you go out to meet him with all the saints in the heavenly kingdom. *(Rite of Christian Initiation of Adults)*[5]

Leader: Let us go forth in peace, rejoicing in the power of God's love to bring his light to all we meet.

All: Amen.

Session Two:
Baptism: The Mystery of Life-Giving Water

Environment: The room is arranged with chairs in a circle to encourage small group discussion. The prayer table is in a prominent spot, and holds a Bible, a large bowl of water, and a candle. For the journey prayer experience, stations have been arranged in nearby rooms if possible. At one station is a large pitcher of chilled water and glasses. Another table holds a bowl of pleasantly scented bath oil. At another station, a table has been placed with enough candles for all of the participants. The sound of running water greets the baptismal ministry team members as they arrive.

Objectives: The catechetical process:

Builds Community:

Encourages people to become better acquainted through the sharing of symbols of self in the introductory activity;

---

5. RCIA, art. 579.

Encourages people to work together to identify the many different uses and meanings of water;

Invites participants to share in small groups a significant life experience with water;

Joins together in a journey prayer experience;

Shares Stories, Beliefs, and Values:

Examines the readings from the Scriptural Lectionary for the *Rite of Baptism of Children* in order to discover the significance of water in the life of God's people;

Helps the group interpret the meaning of water in the celebration of baptism;

Prays Together:

Fosters a spirit of active listening to the Word of God through singing of the "Alleluia" and standing for the Gospel;

Provides the opportunity to prayerfully explore the meaning of other baptismal symbols in a journey prayer experience;

Motivates for Justice:

Examines the Gospel selections for the baptism of children for insights into the manner in which Christians are to live;

Discusses the way in which baptismal ministry should be done in light of the Gospel command to love;

Sensitizes the participants to the implications of service toward others in the prayer texts for the anointing with chrism, clothing with the white garment, and presentation of the lighted candle;

Reminds the catechetical community that the praying of the Lord's Prayer has implications toward action on behalf of justice;

Begins and ends the prayer experience at the table of the Word, challenging people to go forth and live God's word.

Welcome: As people enter, they are given blank name tags. They are asked to choose a marking pen in a color that they like and to draw on their name tag something which best describes them. When all have assembled, each person will take turns sharing the reason for the color and the symbol chosen.

Gathering Prayer: The catechist invites the baptismal ministry team to gather around the prayer table. One member of the group moves to the prayer table and lights the candle as the group joins in singing "You Have Been Baptized in Christ," by Carey Landry.[6]

You Have Been Baptized in Christ

Refrain:
We have been baptized in Christ.
It is he that we have put on.
We who are washed in this water
Have hope of eternal life.

God the Father has freed you and given you a new birth,
And to be a member of his holy people, he now anoints you with oil.
You are a new creation. In Christ you have been clothed.
See in this garment the outward sign of your dignity in him.

Receive the light of Christ; keep it burning brightly.
Always walk as a child of the light, with his flame alive in your heart.

When the song is completed, the lector reverently walks over to the prayer table and picks up the Bible.

Lector: Alleluia

All: Alleluia

Lector: A Reading from the Gospel of John. (Jn. 7:37-39)
On the last and greatest day of the festival, Jesus stood up and cried out: "If anyone thirsts, let that one come to me; let the one drink who believes in me. Scripture has it: 'From within him, rivers of living water shall flow.'"
This is the Gospel of the Lord.

All: Praise to you, Lord Jesus Christ.
Silence

Leader: Loving God, we gather here today as your people, who have been led by faith to you, the fountain of all life. Be present to us, Lord, as we gather in your name. Pour out your loving kindness upon us and bathe us in your grace so that we might become the instruments through which your waters of life are given to others. May our service

---

6. Carey Landry, "You Have Been Baptized in Christ," *Glory and Praise*, vol. 1, (Phoenix, Az.: NALR, 1977) #60.

in baptismal ministry give glory to you, our living and true God, forever and ever.

All: Amen.

Consideration of a Human Experience: The catechist invites team members to sit in a comfortable position, close their eyes, and listen to the following sounds. The catechist plays a tape with a variety of water sounds, such as: rain, thunder and rain, a babbling brook, a mountain stream, a waterfall, a shower, a washing machine, someone washing dishes in the sink, children splashing in a swimming pool, ocean waves, the sea hitting the beach and the rocks.[7] The catechist invites the group to identify the various sounds. After all sounds have been identified, the catechist asks if there are other water sounds that have been left out. The catechist then directs discussion on the following topics:

Did you associate any feelings with the water sounds as you heard them?

What common meanings do people associate with water?

Share one memorable experience that you have had with water.

Faith Reflection: The catechist says, "The Church has always used water to express new life in Christ through the power of the Holy Spirit. It is with water that the Church initiates its new members. Our Scriptures speak to us of the significance of water in the life of God's people. The Lectionary for the *Rite of Baptism for Children* contains some of these significant water stories, and other passages related to baptism. Let us spend some time listening to these stories and discussing them."

The catechist divides team members into small groups of two or three; each small group is given one of the following Scripture passages from the Lectionary for infant baptism:

Ex. 17:3-7 – Water from the rock;

Ez. 36:24-28 – Clean water, a new heart, a renewed spirit;

Gal. 3:26-28 – Now that you have been baptized, you have put on Christ;

Mt. 28:18-20 – Christ sends his apostles to teach and baptize;

Mk. 1:9-11 – The baptism of Jesus;

Mk. 12:28-34 – Love God with all your heart;

---

7. "Sounds of Nature and the Great Outdoors," Compact Disk Audio Recording (Quebec, Canada: AAD) SECD 5504.

Jn. 3:1-6 – The meeting with Nicodemus;

Jn. 4:5-14 – Jesus speaks with a Samaritan woman;

Jn. 7:37-39 – Streams of living water;

Jn. 19:31-35 – The death of Christ, the witness of John the apostle.

The small groups are instructed to read over their passage and to consider in what ways it speaks to them about baptism. After 15 to 20 minutes the group comes back together to share their insights. A short break follows.

At the end of the break the catechist presents each member of the baptismal ministry team with a copy of *The Rite of Baptism for Children,*[8] with the introductory notes, and *Infant Baptism in the Parish: Understanding the Rite.*[9]1 These are resources for team members which they can read over on their own.

Action on Behalf of Justice: The word of God is the link that propels us to the ritual action. The Scriptural Lectionary for the *Rite of Baptism for Children* gives us three different readings proclaiming the commandment to love (Mt. 22:35-40, Mk. 12:28-34 and Jn. 15:1-11). Considering the emphasis that is placed on these passages in the Scriptural Lectionary for the rite, what are the implications for all who are baptized in Christ? What implications might this have for how we do baptismal ministry?

The other symbolic actions of baptism: the anointing with oil, the clothing with the white garment, and the presentation of the baptismal candle, are ritual actions which explain what has happened to us in baptism. Read over the words of the prayer texts for these symbolic actions. What do they say to all of us as baptized Christians about the way we must live? What are the implications in these prayer texts for how we do baptismal ministry?

The prayer texts are as follows:

God the Father of our Lord Jesus has freed you from sin, given you a new birth by water and the Holy Spirit, and welcomed you into his holy people. He now anoints you with the chrism of salvation. As Christ was anointed Priest, Prophet, and King, so may you live always as members of his body, sharing everlasting life.

---

8. *The Rite of Baptism for Children,* (Collegeville, MN: Liturgical Press, 1970).
9. Gabe Huck, *Infant Baptism in the Parish: Understanding the Rite,* (Chicago: Liturgical Training Publications, 1980).

You have become a new creation and have clothed yourselves in Christ. See in this white garment the outward sign of your Christian dignity. With your family and friends to help you by word and example, bring that dignity unstained into the everlasting life of heaven.

Parents and godparents, this light is entrusted to you to be kept burning brightly. These children of yours have been enlightened by Christ. They are to walk always as children of the light. May they keep the flame of faith alive in their hearts. When the Lord comes, may they go out to meet him with all the saints in the heavenly kingdom.[10]

The baptismal liturgy concludes with the Lord's prayer. This prayer is prayed by the assembly in all sacraments. (The Rite of Reconciliation for an individual penitent is the only exception.) What does this prayer say to us about how our actions need to be oriented toward justice?

Closing Prayer: The catechist invites the group to join together in a journeying prayer experience. Each member of the baptismal team has been assigned a role for each stop on the journey. The journey begins at the prayer table, where the catechist holds up the bowl of water saying,

> Leader: My dear sisters and brothers, God uses the sacrament of water to give divine life to those who believe. Let us turn to God, asking that God pour on us the gift of divine life.

A reader continues,

> Reader: Father, you give us grace through sacramental signs which tell of the wonders of your unseen power. In baptism we use your gift of water, which you have made a rich symbol of the grace you have given us in this sacrament.
>
> At the very dawn of creation, your Spirit breathed on the waters, making them the wellspring of all holiness . . . .
> We ask you, Father, with your Son, to send the Holy Spirit upon this water. May all who are buried with Christ in the death of baptism rise also with him to the newness of life.[11]
>
> The catechist places the bowl of water back on the table, picks up the lighted candle from the prayer table, and leads the group to another room where a table has been

---

10. RBC, art. 62, 63, 64.
11. RBC, art. 54.

placed holding a pitcher of chilled spring water and enough glasses for the group. When all have gathered around the table, the catechist places the candle on the table and the prayer leader begins.

Leader: Praise to you, almighty God, for you have created water to refresh, to satisfy, and to give life.

All: Blessed be God

Lector: A reading from the Gospel of John.
Jesus said (to the Samaritan woman), "Everyone who drinks of this water will thirst again, but whoever drinks of the water I shall give will never thirst. The water that I shall give will become a spring of water welling up to eternal life." (Jn. 4:13-14)
This is the Gospel of the Lord.

All: Praise to you, Lord Jesus Christ.

The leader pours and gives a glass of water to one of the baptismal team members. Each person in turn comes forward to pour and give a glass of water to someone else. The last person gives a glass of water to the prayer leader. When all the glasses have been poured, the group drinks together. During the water ritual, a tape of David Haas' song, "Water of Life"[12]4 is played. All join in to sing the refrain.

Water of Life

Refrain:
Water of Life, Jesus our light;
Journey from death to new life. (twice)
Fountain of light, new sight for the blind;
We come to the water, we come now to see.

Fountain of compassion, freedom from fear;
We come to the water, we come to find peace.

Fountain of justice, free all our hate;
We come to the water, we come now to love.

Fountain of mercy, bind all our wounds;
We come to your water, we come to be healed.

Fountain of mission, calling our name;
We come to the water, we come now to serve.

---

12. David Haas, "Water of Life," *As Water to the Thirsty*, (Chicago: GIA Publications, 1987).

The catechist picks up the candle from the prayer table and all journey to the next station, a room with a table containing a bowl of fragrant bath oil. The catechist places the candle on the table, and raises the bowl of oil, as the prayer leader says,

> Leader: Praise to you, God the Holy Spirit, for you anointed Christ at his baptism in the waters of the Jordan, so that we might all be baptized into you.

> All: Blessed be God.

> Leader: Oil applied ahead of time
> seals the skin against its enemies,
> sun and water, wind and cold; . . .
> Oil applied remedially
> repairs the wounds of war and work;
> chapped, cracked, broken skin,
> salved and soothed,
> unguent for bruise and burn,
> for wound and rash, . . .
> poured, smeared, daubed, rubbed in:
> liniment of the spirit,
> healing balm[13]

The leader then extends the bowl of oil to the group and invites each person to come forward to dip his or her fingers in the scented oil. The leader tells the group to touch the oil to the palm of each hand with the other middle finger, a gesture used to signify Jesus. At the conclusion, the catechist picks up the candle and leads the group to another space that has a table with unlighted candles for the group. The catechist places the candle on the table as the prayer leader says,

> Leader: *Lumen Christi!* Light of Christ!

> All: Blessed be God.

> Lector: A reading from the Gospel of John.
> Jesus spoke to them once again: "I am the light of the world. No followers of mine shall ever walk in darkness; now they shall possess the light of life."
> This is the Gospel of the Lord.

> All: Praise to you, Lord Jesus Christ.

---

13. adapted from Mark Searle, "Oil and Chrism," *Assembly*, Vol. 8, No. 1 (September, 1981): 141.

Leader: Out of darkness God has called us,
we are claimed by Christ as God's own people,
a chosen race and royal priesthood,
walking in God's marvelous light.[14]
Each person is invited to take a taper, and light it from
the Christ candle. When all candles are lit, the leader
prays the following petitions.

Leader: That the grace poured out on us at baptism be renewed
in us, we pray to the Lord.

All: Lord hear our prayer.

Leader: That through baptismal ministry we may lead others to
Christ, the light of the world, we pray to the Lord.

All: Lord hear our prayer.

Leader: That we may help parents to become examples of faith
for their children, we pray to the Lord.

All: Lord, hear our prayer.

Leader: For our own needs – (pause for individual petitions) –
we pray to the Lord.

All: Lord, hear our prayer.
The catechist picks up the candle and leads group members carrying their lighted candles back to the original
meeting space, where they gather once again around the
prayer table. The catechist places the candle on the table,
and the prayer leader says,

Leader: Praise to you, Lord Jesus Christ, the Creator's only Son,
for you offered yourself on the cross so that, in the blood
and water flowing from your side and through your
death and resurrection, the Church might be born.

All: Blessed be God.

Leader: At the beginning and end of Mass,
At the beginning and end of our lives,
At the beginning and ending of all we do
stands the sign of the cross, saying:

14. adapted from Christopher Walker, "RCIA: Rites and Music," from the Workshop,
"Bringing Life to the RCIA," Archdiocese of Los Angeles Religious Education Congress,
April 22,1989.

> This place, this space of time, this life,
> this child, these people, this body
> belongs to the Lord and will not be snatched from Him,
> who bears indelibly in his body
> the marks of that same cross.[15]

The catechist raises the bowl of water and invites all to come forward to renew their baptismal pledges by blessing themselves with water, "In the name of the Father, the Son, and the Holy Spirit." At the conclusion of the blessing, the catechist invites the community to join hands and pray together the Lord's Prayer.

All are then invited to share a sign of peace, and to go forth to share life with family, friends, and loved ones.

Session Three: Infant Baptismal Ministry: An Invitation to "Come and See"

Environment: The session takes place in a comfortable meeting room. At the front of the room is a table covered with a white cloth. The following items are placed on the table: a candle, a Bible, a loaf of bread, and a carafe of wine.

Objectives: The Catechetical Process:

Builds Community:

> Identifies in small groups the needs of the people who come for infant baptismal preparation;
>
> Develops some ways in which the baptismal ministry team can meet the needs of parents;
>
> Considers the strengths and weaknesses of the baptismal ministry team;
>
> Invites participants to share bread, wine, and fellowship together through an *agape* meal;

Shares Stories, Beliefs and Values:

> Presents Jesus as a model for ministry through consideration of the story of Jesus' meeting with the woman at the well (Jn. 4:4-42);

---

15. Mark Searle, "Sign of the Cross," *Assembly* Vol. 6, No. 3 (December, 1979): 75.

Examines the ministerial gifts of the catechetical community in light of Paul's Letter to the Romans (Rm. 12:3-8);

Prays Together:

Invites participants to pray and sing together in a breaking-of-the-bread service;

Action on Behalf of Justice:

Considers the ways by which infant baptismal ministers can respect the cultural differences of the parents with whom they work;

Seeks ways to better meet the needs of the community;

Affirms the gifts of the baptismal ministry team and seeks ways to strengthen any weaknesses in the team.

Welcoming: The catechist greets baptismal team members at the door as they arrive. Time is provided for people to mingle and visit. Coffee and refreshments are available. After a suitable amount of time the catechist gathers the group together and formally welcomes them.

Gathering Prayer: The catechist invites the group to gather around the prayer table. One member of the group lights the prayer candles as the group joins in singing "Gather Us In" by Marty Haugen.[16]

Gather Us In

Here in this place, new light is streaming;
Now is the darkness vanished away.
See in this space our fears and our dreamings,
Brought here to you in the light of this day.

Gather us in, the lost and forsaken;
Gather us in, the blind and the lame.
Call to us now, and we shall awaken;
We shall arise at the sound of our name.

When the song is completed, the lector moves to the prayer table and reverently picks up the Bible.

Lector: Alleluia

All: Alleluia

---

16. Marty Haugen, "Gather Us In," from the songbook *Gather Us In*, (Chicago: GIA Publications Inc., 1982).

Lector: A reading from the Gospel according to John. (John 1:35-42)

The next day John was there again with two of his disciples. As he watched Jesus walk by he said, "Look! There is the Lamb of God!" The two disciples heard what he said, and followed Jesus. When Jesus turned around and noticed them following him, he asked them, "What are you looking for?" They said to him, "Rabbi (which means Teacher), where do you stay?" "Come and see," he answered. So they went to see where he was lodged, and stayed with him that day. (It was about four in the afternoon.)

One of the two who had followed him after hearing John was Simon Peter's brother, Andrew. The first thing he did was to seek out his brother Simon and tell him, "We have found the Messiah!" (This term means the Anointed.) He brought him to Jesus, who looked at him and said, "You are Simon, son of John; your name shall be Cephas" (which is rendered Peter.)

This is the Gospel of the Lord.

All: Praise to you Lord Jesus Christ.
Silence

Leader: Lord God, You invite each of us to come and see where you live. As members of your Body, may we also invite others into our midst. Be present to us as we gather this evening in your name. Guide us so that we might become a welcoming people who invite others also to come and see. All glory and praise be yours, Lord Jesus Christ, forever and ever.

All: Amen.

Consideration of a Human Experience: As an exercise, team members are given a demographic profile. The profile should typify the ethnicity, economic and educational status of the parish in which they minister. The baptismal ministry team is divided into small groups, given butcher paper and marking pens, and asked to discuss and write down five parental needs revealed in the profile that a baptismal preparation ministry would need to address in the sample parish.

Sample Parish Profile of Parents of Children to be Baptized

    Parish: Name

Name of Program:
    Catechesis for Infant Baptism

Approximate number in the program:
    15 to 20; representing 6 to 8 families,
    the parents and often the godparents;

    Age: Between 18 - 40 (young adults) Most are in their mid-twenties;

    Ethnicity: Filipino 50%
    Hispanic 20%
    Anglo 0%

    Sex: Almost evenly divided between men and women, as both spouses are required to attend catechetical sessions;
    Family Status:

Out of 8 families, typically:
    one couple is unmarried;
    three couples are not married in the Church;
    four couples were married in the Church;
    for five couples, this is the first child;
    for three couples, this child has older siblings;

Level of Education:
    In general, unknown. Most appear to have at least a high school education;
    All speak English, although many may not understand the nuances of English phrases;

Special Needs:
    Those unmarried or not married in the church may be sensitive to their status within the Church;
    Some speak English with an accent. May be unwilling to share ideas in large group;
    Some may be in mixed marriages – Catholic and another religious affiliation;
    Some are military personnel and therefore transient;
    At least one couple will never have been fully initiated into Church (no eucharist or confirmation);

   Occasionally some may have difficulty reading or write
in English;
Parish Participation: Most participants have young families and are not very involved in parish life;
Many do not regularly attend Mass;
Some cradle Catholics may be very traditional;
Some may feel alienated from the Church; others are just
returning to the practice of their faith;
Some may be hostile to the program and resent the man-
datory class requirement;
After about twenty minutes, the catechist brings the
groups back together to compare and prioritize the lists
of needs.

Faith Reflection: Jesus invited Andrew and Peter and the others to "come
and see." He invited a man born blind to "come and see." Here is still
another story of one who was invited to "come and see."

   The lector walks over to the prayer table and picks up the Bible.
Two others join the lector to proclaim the Gospel in dialogue.[17]

   Readers: Narrator, Jesus, Samaritan Woman

   Narr: Alleluia

    All: Alleluia

   Narr: A Reading from the Gospel of John. (Jn. 4:4-42)

   Narr: Jesus had to pass through Samaria and he came to a city
     of Samaria called Sychar, near the field that Jacob gave
     to his son Joseph. Jacob's well was there, and so Jesus,
     wearied as he was with his journey, sat down beside the
     well. It was about the sixth hour.
     There came a woman of Samaria to draw water. Jesus
     said to her,

   Jesus: Give me a drink.

   Narr: For his disciples had gone away into the city to buy food.
     The Samaritan woman said to him,

  Woman: How is it that you, a Jew, ask a drink of me, a woman
     of Samaria?

---

17. Richard Chilson, *A Lenten Pilgrimage*, (Ramsey, N.J.: Paulist, 1983) 61-63.

Narr: For Jews had no dealings with Samaritans.

Jesus: If you knew the gift of God, and who it is that is saying to you, "Give me a drink," you would have asked him, and he would have given you living water.

Woman: Sir, you have nothing to draw with, and the well is deep. Where will you get that living water? Are you greater than our father, Jacob, who gave us the well and drank from it himself, and his sons, and his cattle?

Jesus: Everyone who drinks of this water will thirst again, but whoever drinks of the water I shall give will never thirst. The water that I shall give will become a spring of water welling up to eternal life.

Woman: Sir, give me this water, that I may not thirst, nor come here to draw.

Jesus: Go, call your husband and come here.

Woman: I have no husband.

Jesus: You are right in saying, "I have no husband," for you have had five husbands, and he whom you now have is not your husband; this you said truly.

Woman: Sir, I perceive that you are a prophet. Our fathers worshipped on this mountain; and you say that Jerusalem is the place where we ought to worship.

Jesus: Woman, believe me, the hour is coming when neither on this mountain nor in Jerusalem will you worship God. You worship what you do not know; we worship what we know, for salvation is from the Jews. But the hour is coming, and now is, when the true worshipers will worship the Father in spirit and truth, for the Father seeks such as these to worship him. God is spirit, and those who worship God must worship in spirit and truth.

Woman: I know that the Messiah is coming; when he comes, he will show us all things.

Jesus: I who speak to you am he.

Narr: Just then his disciples came. They marveled that he was talking with a woman, but none said, "What do you wish?" or "Why are you talking with her?" So the woman left her water jar, went away into the city, and said to the people,

Woman: Come, see a man who told me all that I ever did. Can this be the Christ?

Narr: Many Samaritans from that city believed in him because of the woman's testimony. "He told me all that I ever did." So when the Samaritans came to him, they asked him to stay with them; and he stayed there two days. And many more believed because of his word. They said to the woman, "It is no longer because of your words that we believe, for we have heard for ourselves, and we know that this is indeed the Savior of the world."[18]9

Narr: This is the Gospel of the Lord.

All: Praise to you, Lord Jesus Christ.

At the conclusion of the Gospel, the catechist asks the group to discuss the following questions.

What were the qualities in Jesus that attracted the Samaritan woman to him?

What needs did Jesus recognize in the Samaritan woman?

How did he meet those needs?

The woman at the well was of a different culture than Jesus; in fact she was from a group that was considered outcasts by the Jews. How did Jesus respect her culture?

Our parish is composed of people from a variety of cultural traditions. How can baptismal preparation ministry respect the differences in cultural understanding?

In what ways can we model our approach to the parents we meet in baptismal ministry after the example of Jesus?

Action on Behalf of Justice: As a baptismal ministry team, we represent the faith community as we invite others to Christ, especially those who experience themselves as somewhat isolated from parish life, those we often call "marginal" Catholics.

In what ways does our group invite others to "come and see"?

---

18. Richard Chilson, *A Lenten Pilgrimage*, (Ramsey, N.J.: Paulist, 1983) 61-63.

What are three attitudes present in this group that might send the wrong message – that might be obstacles for those we deal with?

In what ways can this baptismal ministry team work to make this ministry one that more readily exemplifies the inviting Spirit of Christ?

What qualities are needed within the baptismal ministry team in order to meet the needs of the parents who come to us?

Many of these qualities are already present within our catechetical community. Scripture tells us something about the gifts that are present within the faith community. Let us listen to the word of God.

A Reading from the Letter of Paul to the Romans. (Rm. 12:3-8)

Do not think of yourselves more highly than you should. Instead, be modest in your thinking, and judge yourselves according to the amount of faith that God has given you. We have many parts in one body, and all these parts have different functions. In the same way, though we are many, we are one body in union with Christ and we are all joined to each other as different parts of one body, So we are to use our different gifts in accordance with the grace that God has given us. If our gift is to speak God's message, we must do it according to the faith that we have. If it is to serve, we must serve. If it is to teach, we must teach. If it is to encourage others, we must do so. Whoever shares what he or she has with others must do it generously; whoever has authority must work hard; whoever shows kindness to others must do it cheerfully.

As a catechetical community, we are blessed with many gifts. Let us consider some of them now. The participants are given a worksheet so they can assess their own ministerial gifts. The catechist directs the group to another room and gives them ten minutes to work individually on the worksheet. While they are working individually, the main room is prepared for the closing prayer service. After completing the following worksheet, group members discuss the gifts present in the baptismal ministry team as well as the areas which need to be strengthened. Suggestions are solicited future training sessions.

Closing Prayer: The tables in the meeting room are arranged in the shape of a cross. In the center is placed a loaf of bread and a carafe of wine. A lighted candle and the Bible are nearby. Cards have been placed on the seats throughout the room for people to read. The group enters the room; one of the catechists will be the prayer leader, and says,

Leader: The initial act of a Jewish meal is the breaking of bread. The early Christians shared this tradition in their homes. It was a sign of community. Today we too will break bread and share it with one another, remembering that we are community.

Jesus of Nazareth invites you to break bread with your brothers and sisters, your friends and neighbors gathered here. Let us join together in singing verses three and four of a gathering hymn.

Leader: Lord Jesus, we come together to share our gifts. Help us to realize the real meaning of bread and wine; just as this food is nourishment for our bodies, so the eucharistic bread and wine nourish our spirits.

Lector: A Reading from the Gospel of John (Jn. 6:32-35, 51)

Jesus said to them: "I solemnly assure you, it was not Moses who gave you bread from the heavens; it is my Father who gives you the real heavenly bread. God's bread comes down from heaven and give life to the world." "Sir, give us this bread always," they besought him. Jesus explained to them: "I myself am the bread of life. No one who comes to me shall ever be hungry, no one who believes in me shall ever thirst. . . . The one who eats this bread shall live forever."

This is the Gospel of the Lord.

All: Praise to you, Lord Jesus Christ.

The bread is passed around the table, as a symbol of the talents of the faith community. All are asked to hold the bread in their hands while the leader prays:

Leader: We share this bread with each other as a sign of our sharing of life with one another through our Lord Jesus Christ.

All: Amen.

Each person is now invited to eat the bread and drink the wine.

Prayers of the Community:

> The response is: Lord, help us to become bread for others.

Reader: God, grant us the freedom to move into the unknown.

All: Lord, help us to become bread for others.

Reader: Give us strength to explore the untried; give us the vision to see the opportunities of each new day.

All: Lord, help us to become bread for others.

Reader: Help us to know that there is no place, no event, no meeting which we enter alone. You are with us.

All: Lord, help us to become bread for others.

Reader: Grace us with the gifts we need to serve you through our ministry of baptismal catechesis. Give us the gifts of authority, kindness, encouragement, generosity, speaking, teaching, and serving.

All: Lord, help us to become bread for others.

Reader: For our own intentions . . .

All: Lord, help us to become bread for others.

Leader: Almighty God, source of all creation, you have made us in your image. Help us to welcome with love all those we meet each day. Let them see in us the words of Christ that renew people; the power and grace of Christ that refashion people. Let those who see us see the likeness of Christ, who lives and reigns forever and ever.[19]

All: Amen.

> The catechetical community continues to enjoy bread, wine and fellowship.

Evaluation of Baptismal Ministry Team Formation

The catechetical sessions for baptismal team ministry formation may be evaluated by comparing how well or how poorly the catechetical objec-

---

19. Adapted from Cullen Schippe, "Hospitality Prayer," *Planting, Watering, Growing: The Volunteer Catechist's Companion,* (Granada Hills Ca.: Sandleprints Publishing, 1990) 78.

tives for the sessions were implemented. The following form evaluates the objectives for the three catechetical sessions.

Please circle the appropriate number below each question.

4 - excellent   3 - good   2 - fair   1 - poor

The Catechetical Process:

Builds Community:

Invites team members to become acquainted through a community building activity.
4 - excellent   3 - good   2 - fair   1 - poor

Encourages people to share in small groups some of their life experiences.
4 - excellent   3 - good   2 - fair   1 - poor

Explores baptismal ministry as a communal process facilitated by the baptismal ministry team.
4 - excellent   3 - good   2 - fair   1 - poor

Encourages people to become better acquainted through the sharing of symbols of self in the introductory activity.
4 - excellent   3 - good   2 - fair   1 - poor

Encourages people to work together to identify the many different uses and meanings of water for life.
4 - excellent   3 - good   2 - fair   1 - poor

Invites participants to share in small groups a significant life experience with water.
4 - excellent   3 - good   2 - fair   1 - poor

Joins together in a journey prayer experience.
4 - excellent   3 - good   2 - fair   1 - poor

Identifies in small groups the needs of a sampling of the people who come for infant baptismal preparation.
4 - excellent   3 - good   2 - fair   1 - poor

Develops some ways in which the baptismal ministry team can meet the needs of parents.
4 - excellent   3 - good   2 - fair   1 - poor

Considers the strengths and weaknesses of the baptismal ministry team.
4 - excellent   3 - good   2 - fair   1 - poor

Invites participants to share bread, wine, and fellowship together through an *agape.*
4 - excellent   3 - good   2 - fair   1 - poor

Shares Stories, Beliefs, and Values:
4 - excellent   3 - good   2 - fair   1 - poor
Encourages participants to reflect on the life experiences that have made them aware of the presence or absence of God in their lives.
4 - excellent   3 - good   2 - fair   1 - poor

Enables the team to recognize that they are members of a believing community, the Church, who through baptism have been empowered by Christ.
4 - excellent   3 - good   2 - fair   1 - poor

Invites team members to reflect on and discuss the images of light and belief in the Gospel of
4 - excellent   3 - good   2 - fair   1 - poor

John 9:1-41 (Jesus cures a blind man).
4 - excellent   3 - good   2 - fair   1 - poor

Examines the readings from the Scriptural Lectionary for the *Rite of Baptism of Children* in order to discover the significance of water in the life of God's people.
4 - excellent   3 - good   2 - fair   1 - poor

Helps the group interpret the meaning of water in the celebration of baptism.
4 - excellent   3 - good   2 - fair   1 - poor

Presents Jesus as a model for ministry through consideration of the story of Jesus' meeting with the woman at the well (Jn. 4:4-42).
4 - excellent   3 - good   2 - fair   1 - poor
Examines the ministerial gifts of the catechetical community in light of Paul's Letter to the Romans (Rm. 12:3-8). 4 - excellent 3 - good   2 - fair   1 - poor

Prays Together:
Provides opportunities for the baptismal team to gather as a community of believers to pray and sing together.
4 - excellent   3 - good   2 - fair   1 - poor

Commissions the members of the baptismal ministry team through a service of light.

4 - excellent   3 - good   2 - fair   1 - poor

Invites different members of the baptismal ministry team to actively participate in the prayer experiences as readers.
4 - excellent   3 - good   2 - fair   1 - poor

Fosters a spirit of active listening to the Word of God through singing of the "Alleluia" and standing for the Gospel.
4 - excellent   3 - good   2 - fair   1 - poor

Provides the opportunity to prayerfully explore the meaning of other baptismal symbols in a journey prayer experience.
4 - excellent   3 - good   2 - fair   1 - poor

Invites participants to pray and sing together in a breaking-of-the-bread service.
4 - excellent   3 - good   2 - fair   1 - poor

Motivates for Justice:

Identifies ways in which the baptismal team will help members of the parish community through the ministry of baptismal catechesis.
4 - excellent   3 - good   2 - fair   1 - poor

Suggests ways in which team members can encourage and support one another in baptismal ministry.
4 - excellent   3 - good   2 - fair   1 - poor

Experiences this ministry team as a community of believers empowered by Christ and commissioned to share faith with others.
4 - excellent   3 - good   2 - fair   1 - poor

Examines the Gospel selections for the baptism of children for insights into the manner in which Christians are to live.
4 - excellent   3 - good   2 - fair   1 - poor
Discusses the way in which baptismal ministry should be done in light of the Gospel command to love.
4 - excellent   3 - good   2 - fair   1 - poor

Sensitizes the participants to the implications of service to others in the prayer texts for the anointing with chrism, clothing with the white garment, and presentation of the lighted candle.
4 - excellent   3 - good   2 - fair   1 - poor

Reminds the catechetical community that the Lord's Prayer has implications toward action on behalf of justice.
4 - excellent   3 - good   2 - fair   1 - poor

Begins and ends the prayer experience at the table of the Word, challenging people to go forth and live God's word.
4 - excellent   3 - good   2 - fair   1 - poor

Considers the ways by which infant baptismal ministry team members can respect the cultural differences of the parents with whom they work.
4 - excellent   3 - good   2 - fair   1 - poor

Seeks ways to better meet the needs of the catechetical community with whom we work.
4 - excellent   3 - good   2 - fair   1 - poor

Affirms the gifts of the baptismal ministry team, and seeks ways to strengthen the weaknesses in the team.
4 - excellent   3 - good   2 - fair   1 - poor

Session Evaluation

After each catechetical session, baptismal team members are asked to turn in a written evaluation of the session, responding to the following questions.

What were the strengths of this session?

What will you remember about this evening?

What could have been left out?

What changes would improve the session?

Other Comments:

Conclusion

In "Symbols Are Actions, Not Objects," Nathan Mitchell says:

> Symbols are not things people invent and interpret, but realities that "make" and interpret a people. What we need today is not so much "better symbols," but a willingness to let ourselves be grasped and explored by them. For a symbol is not an object to be manipulated through mime and memory, but an environment to be inhabited. Symbols are places to live, breathing spaces that help us discover the possibilities that life offers.[1]

Through the Word proclaimed and heard, gesture, and ritual action, the symbols of baptism "make and interpret" God's people, the Church. The symbols of baptism invite us to enter into the sacrament and to be transformed into God's own people.

Symbols "help us to discover the possibilities that life offers." They give us new insights into our human experiences and into our relationships with other people. In this book, we have examined the *Rite of Baptism for Children* in its prayer texts, scriptural lectionary, and use of symbols. As we attempt to interpret this fundamental sacrament of Christian life, we may discover that we have been interpreted as well.

In grappling with the baptismal rite, we find that we approach baptism with new eyes. We are more keenly aware that the symbols of baptism call us into deeper relationship with other people as members of Christ's body, for the baptismal liturgy speaks most clearly of each person as graced before God. Therefore each person that one encounters in baptismal ministry is to be treated with respect and dignity. We can now approach baptismal catechesis with the realization that the symbols of baptism must be entered into fully, in order that we might experience in the sacramental celebration what David Power calls "the mystery of

---

1. Nathan Mitchell, "'Symbols are Actions, Not Objects' – New Directions for an Old Problem," *Living Worship*, 13 (February 1977).

God revealing himself in Christ made present in the community in and through its symbols."[2] We are more deeply aware of the transformative power of baptism and its symbols when we allow ourselves to enter into them fully.

It is my hope that this resource for baptismal team ministry preparation will enable your faith community to become a more welcoming presence to families who come for baptism. If we, as members of various baptismal ministry teams, open ourselves to the richness of the baptismal symbols and allow them to transform us, through our ministry parishes may experience God's presence in all people. May the Holy Spirit, who makes holy all creation, enable this ministry to bear much fruit within your faith community!

2.   Power, 175.

APPENDIX 1: GOSPEL ANALYSIS

GOSPEL	FORM	REFERENCE TO SYMBOLIC ACTION	IMAGE OF GOD	RELATIONSHIP TO COMMUNITY	THEME OF READING	OTHER INSIGHTS
Matthew 22:35-40	Saying of Jesus		Jesus Lord, Your God	The Church is called to a total commitment of love for God and for the neighbor as oneself	The greatest commandment is love	All of God's law is a law in obedience to love.
Matthew 28:18-20	Saying of Jesus	The baptismal formula, "Baptize them in the name of the Father, and of the Son, and of the Holy Spirit"	Jesus, in full authority; leading and commissioning his disciples to go and teach; as remaining always with them Father, Son and Spirit	We are a Church of the baptized. The The presence of Christ is always with us Through baptism we become disciples.	The commission of the Apostles.	
Mark 1:9-11	Narrative	Baptism in the river Jordan. Water and the Spirit	Jesus. The Spirit like a dove. Voice from heaven. Father and beloved Son.	Jesus is baptized. The Father claims him as son. Through baptism we are children of God.	The baptism of Jesus.	
Mark 10:13-16	Narrative	Jesus calls the children to himself; blesses them, lays hands on them.	Jesus, indignant with the apostles; embracing, blessing the children.	The Kingdom of God belongs to the child-like.	Jesus blesses the little children.	Parents and all the Church are to allow and encourage these little ones to come to Jesus. The Church is called to have the receptivity of children, making no claims to power or status.

GOSPEL	FORM	REFERENCE TO SYMBOLIC ACTION	IMAGE OF GOD	RELATIONSHIP TO COMMUNITY	THEME OF READING	OTHER INSIGHTS
Jn. 4:5-14	Narrative Discourse	living water, flowing water, water from which one will never be thirsty, fountain of eternal life.	Jesus, a Jew, tired and thirsty, who speaks to Samaritans and women, God's gift, who gives living water, greater than Jacob, who gives the water of eternal life.	We come to the Lord for the water of eternal life, the living waters of baptism.	Jesus meets a Samaritan woman; the need we have for the living water Jesus gives.	
Jn. 9:1-7	Narrative Discourse	I am the light of the world, washing in water – comes back able to see, enligtened	Jesus, the light of the world, who gives sight to the blind; God'sworks shown forth.	All washed in the waters of baptism are given new sight, enlightened in Christ.	Jesus heals a man born blind.	The washing gave him his sight through which he became a new person – a new creation.
Jn. 19:31-35	Narrative	blood and water flowed out from his side	Jesus, who died the cross, whose side waspierced by a lance from which flowed blood and water	All who are baptized, are baptized into Jesus' death.	Blood and water.	Those who are washed in the waters of baptism, experience the pouring out of the Spirit of Jesus upon them so that they might come into new life with Christ.

Appendix 2: Prayer Text Analysis

PRAYER TEXT	ADDRESS	NAME OF GOD	DESCRIPTION	DEEDS OF GOD	NAME OF JESUS
49b Almighty God	God the Father	God Father	almighty and everlasting	You sent your only Son	only Son Christ our Lord
54a Father You	God the Father	God, Father	your unseen power	you give grace through sacramental signs; you make water a rich symbol of grace you give in this sacrament; you made the waters of the great flood a sign of baptism, making an end to sin and new beginning to goodness; you led Israel out of slavery; you created man in your own likeness.	you Son, Christ our Lord
60 Is it	community	Father, Son and Holy Spirit			the Son
62 God the	children	God the Father		anoints the baptized with the chrism of salvation; gives a new birth; frees from sin; welcomes you into his holy people.	our Lord, Jesus Christ; priest, prophet, king

Prayer Text Analysis

JESUS' RELATIONSHIP TO THE CHURCH	REFERENCE TO PASCHAL MYSTERY	NAME OF SPIRIT	WORKS OF THE SPIRIT	NAME OF CHURCH	BLESSINGS OF CHURCH
To rescue us from the slavery of sin; to give us the freedom of sons and daughters.	You son died and rose again to save us; his victory over sin and death.				Bring these children out of the power of darkness; strengthen them with the grace of Christ; watch over them at every step of life's journey.
Was baptized by John, anointed with the Spirit; sent his disciples to teach and baptize in the name of the Trinity.	Willed that water and blood should flow from his side as he hung upon the cross; May all who are buried with Christ in the death of baptism rise with him to newness of life.	Your Spirit, the Holy Spirit	Breathed on the waters making them the well-spring of all holiness; anoints; gives to the water the grace of Christ; cleanse from sin and bring to new birth of innocence.	We who use your gift of water; God's holy people, set free from sin by baptism; Your Church; all who are buried with Christ in baptism, rise to new life.	Look now with live upon your Church and unseal for her the fountain of all baptism; Give to the water the grace of your son, cleanse us from sin in in a new birth to innocence; may all who die with Christ in baptism be brought to newness of life.
		Holy Spirit		the Church	to be baptized in the faith of the Church in the name of the Father, Son and Spirit.
His body		Holy Spirit and water		His holy people; members of his body.	That we may live always as members of his body sharing everlasting life.

Selected Bibliography

Baker, J. Robert, Nyberg, Larry J., and Tufano, Victoria M., ed. *A Baptism Sourcebook.* Chicago: Liturgy Training Publications, 1993.

Brady, Joan, and William Koplik. *We Celebrate Baptism.* Morristown, N.J.: Silver Burdett, 1983.

Brown, Kathy, and Frank Sokol, ed. *Issues in the Christian Initiation of Children: Catechesis and Liturgy.* Chicago: Liturgy Training Publications, 1989.

Brown, Raymond, Joseph Fitzmyer, S.J., Roland E. Murphy, O. Carm., ed. *The New Jerome Biblical Commentary.* New Jersey: Prentice Hall, 1990.

Catechesis and Mystagogy: Infant Baptism, video. Allen, TX: Tabor Publishing Co. Not yet published.

Champlin, Joseph. *The Marginal Catholic: Challenge Don't Crush.* Notre Dame, Indiana: Ave Maria Press, 1989.

Chilson, Richard. *A Lenten Pilgrimage.* Ramsey, N.J.: Paulist, 1983.

Committee on Marriage and Family life. *A Family Perspective in Church and Society: A Manual For All Pastoral Leaders.* Washington, D.C.: United States Catholic Conference, 1988.

Dooley, Kate. "The Sign of the Cross." *Liturgy* 7 (Summer 1987): 61-67.

Fitzgerald, Timothy. *Infant Baptism: A Parish Celebration.* Chicago: Liturgy Training Publications, 1994.

Foltz, Nancy, ed. *Handbook of Adult Religious Education.* Birmingham, Alabama: Religious Education Press, 1986.

Gallagher, Maureen. "Forming Today's Disciples: Five Emerging Trends in Adult Catechesis." *New Catholic World* 230 (September/October 1987): 196-201.

Gallagher, Rosemary, and John Trenchard, C.SS.R. *Your Baby's Baptism.* Liguori, Ms.: Liguori Publications, 1985.

Hinman, Karen. *How to Form a Catechumenate Team.* Chicago: Liturgy Training Publications, 1986.

Huck, Gabe. *Infant Baptism in the Parish: Understanding the Rite.* Chicago: Liturgy Training Publications, 1980.

Karay, Diane. "Let the Children Lead the Way: A Case for Baptizing Children." *Worship* 61 (July 1987): 336-349.

Kavanagh, Aidan. *The Shape of Baptism: the Rite of Christian Initiation.* New York: Pueblo, 1978.

Kelly, Maureen. "Shaping Parent Sacramental Programs for the Future." *New Catholic World* 230 (September/October 1987): 202-204.

Lane, Dermot. *The Experience of God: An Invitation to Do Theology.* Ramsey, N.J.: Paulist, 1981.

Levad, Karen. "Meeting Parents Needs in a Pre-baptismal Program." *Pace 12.* Winona, Mn.: Saint Mary's Press, 1981-82: Approaches-E.

_____. "Following Through After Baptismal Preparation Programs: Ministry to Developing Families." *Pace 15.* Winona, Mn.: Saint Mary's Press, 1984-85: Approaches-M.

Madden-Connor, Therese. "Preparing Parents for Baptism." *Catechist* (January 1990): 28-29.

Mitchell, Nathan. "'Symbols Are Actions, Not Objects' - New Directions for an Old Problem." *Living Worship* 13 (February 1977).

Mongoven, Anne Marie. *Signs of Catechesis.* New York: Paulist, 1979.

_____. "Catechists and Liturgists: Can We Bring Them Together?." *PACE 15.* Winona, Mn.: St. Mary's Press, 1984-85.

National Advisory Committee on Adult Religious Education (NA-CARE). *Serving Life and Faith: Adult Religious Education and the Adult Catholic Community.* Washington D.C.: Department of Education, United States Catholic Conference, 1986.

National Conference of Catholic Bishops. *Sharing the Light of Faith: National Catechetical Directory for Catholics of the United States.* Washington D.C.: United States Catholic Conference, Department of Education, 1979.

Nowell, Irene. "Biblical Images of Water." *Liturgy* 7 (Summer 1987): 41-45.

Osborne, Kenan, O.F.M.A. *The Christian Sacraments of Initiation.* Mahwah, N.J.: Paulist Press, 1987.

Ostdiek, Gilbert. *Catechesis for Liturgy.* Washington, D.C.: Pastoral Press, 1986.

Parent, Neil, ed. *Agenda for the 90s.* Washington D.C.: Department of Education, United States Catholic Conference, 1989.

Power, David. "The Mystery Which is Worship." *Living Light* 16 (Summer 1979): 168-178.

Rahner, Karl. *A Rahner Reader.* Gerald McCool, ed. New York: Seabury Press, 1975.

Ramshaw, Gail. *Words Around the Font.* Chicago: Liturgy Training Publications, 1994.

Reynolds, Brian. *A Chance to Serve: Peer Ministers' Handbook.* Winona, Mn.: Saint Mary's Press, 1984.

"The Rite of Baptism for Children." *The Rites of the Catholic Church.* New York: Pueblo, 1983.

The Rite of Christian Initiation of Adults. Washington D.C.: United States Catholic Conference, 1988.

Sawner, Marvin. "How is Faith Formed? A Group Dynamics Exercise." *Pace 15.* Winona, Mn.: Saint Mary's Press, 1984-85: Approaches-K.

Scannell, Anthony. *Baptism: Your Child and You.* Los Angeles: Franciscan Communications, 1988.

Schippe, Cullen. *Planting, Watering, Growing: The Volunteer Catechist's Companion.* Granada hills, Ca.: Sandleprints Publishing, 1990.

Searle, Mark, documentation and commentary. *The Church Speaks about Sacraments with Children.* Chicago: Liturgy Training Publications, 1990.

Searle, Mark, ed. "Liturgical Gestures." *Assembly* 6 (December 1979) 74-79.

Stevick, Daniel. "The Water of Life." *Liturgy* 7 (Summer 1987): 47-55.

Szentkeresti, Karen, and Jeanne Tighe. *Rethinking Adult Religious Education: A Practical Parish Guide.* New York: Paulist, 1986.

Tufano, Victoria, ed. *Readings in the Christian Initiation of Children.* Chicago: Liturgy Training Publications, 1994.

Vaillancourt, Patricia, M.A. *Baptism: Your Child's New Life in Christ*. Allen, TX: Tabor Publishing. Not yet published.

Warren, Michael, ed. *Sourcebook for Modern Catechetics*. Winona, Mn.: Saint Mary's Press, 1983.

Wilde, James A., ed. *Before and After Baptism: the Work of Teachers and Catechists*. Chicago: Liturgy Training Publications, 1988.